THE MIRROR OF GOD

Christian Faith as Spiritual Practice
Lessons from Buddhism
and Psychotherapy

JAMES W. JONES

palgrave
macmillan

THE MIRROR OF GOD
Copyright © James W. Jones, 2003.
All rights reserved. No part of this book may be used or reproduced in any manner whatsoever without written permission except in the case of brief quotations embodied in critical articles or reviews.

First published 2003 by
PALGRAVE MACMILLAN™
175 Fifth Avenue, New York, N.Y. 10010 and
Houndmills, Basingstoke, Hampshire, England RG21 6XS.
Companies and representatives throughout the world.

PALGRAVE MACMILLAN is the global academic imprint of the Palgrave Macmillan division of St. Martin's Press, LLC and of Palgrave Macmillan Ltd. Macmillan® is a registered trademark in the United States, United Kingdom and other countries. Palgrave is a registered trademark in the European Union and other countries.

ISBN 1–4039–6102–6 hardback
Library of Congress Cataloging-in-Publication Data
Jones, James William, 1943-
The mirror of God : Christian faith as spiritual practice / James W. Jones.
     p.   cm.
  Includes bibliographical references and index.
  ISBN 1–4039–6102–6
  1. Spirituality.   2. Christianity—Psychology.   3. Buddhism—Relations—Christianity.   4. Christianity and other religions—Buddhism.
I. Title.

BV4501.3.J65   2003
248.4—dc21
                                                    2003042891

A catalogue record for this book is available from the British Library.

Design by Letra Libre, Inc.

First edition: November 2003
10   9   8   7   6   5   4   3   2   1

Printed in the United States of America.

For Kathleen

Contents

Acknowledgements

This book began as a series of lectures on spirituality and psychotherapy that I was invited to give at the Mountain Area Health Education Center in Asheville, North Carolina, in 1997. Over the ensuing years these lectures were continually revised and presented in a variety of religious and professional settings including the Center for Psychotherapy, Education, and Spiritual Growth in Oklahoma City, Oklahoma, in 2000. They also formed the basis for courses on spirituality and counseling that I taught at Union Theological Seminary in New York and Drew Theological Seminary in New Jersey. I want to thank all those who invited me to deliver these lectures and the many colleagues and students who provided valuable feedback and suggestions.

Professors Chung-fang Yu and Franz Metcalf carefully read and extensively critiqued the sections on Buddhism. Their hard work improved the clarity and accuracy of my discussion but any inaccuracies and misinterpretations of Buddhism that remain are entirely my responsibility.

This book grows directly out of a life lived on the boundary between spiritual practice and the practice of psychotherapy. Walking a tightrope between these two disciplines, as well as the rest of my life, has become much more gracious and joyful in the last few years because of the companionship of Kathleen Bishop. Our continual conversations and shared interest in the topic of this book have enriched and deepened not only this text but also my entire life.

Introduction

New York City is full of churches: oases of calm amid the cacophony of blaring horns, shrieking sirens, rumbling and rattling subway trains. Recently a frantic New Yorker confessed to me that she longed to enter one of those gray granite and marble Gothic edifices and simply sit in a pew and absorb the peace she knew was there. But she couldn't, she said. She couldn't because she didn't believe everything the church taught.

How sad, I thought, that she deprived herself of the tranquility she desperately needed because she felt she couldn't believe something. And how could she ever come to believe anything more unless she was willing to do something more?

The heart of this book is the insistence that understanding requires doing. And understanding something new requires doing something new. A deeper spirituality requires a deeper spiritual practice.

Another conviction (demonstrated in decades of working with people) on which this book rests is that if you begin a spiritual practice and stick with it, you will discover new spiritual realities. Spiritual truth is not something to passively accept or mindlessly believe. Spiritual wisdom is for you to discover for yourself. Your practices are the means of this discovery.

This point, that Christian spirituality starts with practice and experience (rather than with, say, belief), is bound to be controversial. But it is, I think, the best way for us to approach the topic and its relevance for our daily lives.

Christian faith is really Christian practice: not trying to pretend to agree with concepts that make no sense to you; not straining to impose a code of conduct on your life that you know in advance you can never live up to. Rather, it is doing things that awaken or deepen the experience of the presence of God.

Why another book on spiritual practice?, you might well ask. Aren't there enough already? What is different about this one?

This book is written from the standpoint of one primarily involved in Christian devotion. But I was trained in the discipline of religious studies and am a professor of religion at a secular state university with colleagues who include Hindus, Moslems, and Chinese and Japanese Buddhists. I have studied and taught a diversity of religious traditions, and have had firsthand encounters with Buddhist practices. So I seek to practice Christianity with an awareness of other religions. As will soon become clear, I think Christians can learn much about the spiritual journey from other traditions and, in my case, especially from Buddhism.

I also think other traditions have much to learn from Christianity. I approach the topic of spiritual practice from a world religions perspective rather than from the perspective of devotional Christianity, or Buddhism, or Hinduism alone. My hope is that whatever your religious tradition, or even if you belong to no tradition, you can find here new insights into the spiritual journey and the role of practice within it.

I also have a doctorate in clinical psychology and have written books and articles about psychotherapy and have worked as a therapist in college counseling centers, in a maximum security prison, in a working-class city, and in a suburban private practice. And I continue to teach and practice as a clinical psychologist. Since this book is written by a practicing psychotherapist, many of the examples and illustrations come from the work of psychotherapy. But many of the lessons learned in this kind of work have relevance beyond the walls of the doctor's office.

Every author has an audience in mind when he or she writes a book. This book is written for you if you are a person who is fascinated with the growing interest in spirituality in our culture—perhaps your own interest or those of people you see around you, and you want to know more about what it might mean for you.

You may have belonged to a religious tradition all your life or you may not affiliate with any tradition or group. But you still find yourself interested in what you hear or see about spiritual practice.

Maybe you find yourself intrigued by the idea of meditation or some other discipline but are not sure what that interest really means.

You may be a committed Buddhist or Hindu practitioner or devout Christian or Moslem believer and you are wondering how your spirituality might be deepened or might affect more of your life.

Or perhaps you are involved in psychotherapy, either as a therapist or a patient or both, and you've heard that spiritual practices might be psychologically beneficial, and wonder if that is really true. And if it is true, what that really means.

Perhaps you saw a TV program about Tibetan lamas, or you recently ordered a book on how to meditate, or bought a CD of Gregorian chants from a Catholic monastery, or attended an adult education class on Zen Buddhist meditation, or a workshop on visualization based on the Kabbala. Or perhaps you go to church on Sunday mornings, or attend a small group that prays for the sick. You may have firsthand experience with a variety of such practices and want to understand more deeply a process you have been engaged in for some time.

Such is the audience I wish for this book.

The last few decades have seen an unexpected explosion of interest not only in spirituality but also in its possible connections with psychology and psychotherapy. Books are being published, conferences scheduled, lectures delivered all across the country on spirituality and psychotherapy. This makes sense in a culture in which psychological terms have become part of our everyday language, and psychological ways of thinking permeate all aspects of our life. A politician gets into trouble and we immediately want to psychoanalyze him. A criminal commits a heinous act and we look to his childhood for an explanation. We feel dissatisfied with our lives and we seek out psychotherapy in record numbers.

Religion and spirituality are not exempt from these trends in our culture. It is only natural that when we approach the topic of spirituality today we often do so in the language of psychology.

In addition, it is no secret that since the late 1960s, churches and other religious institutions have declined significantly in their strength and importance in American life. In the nineties this decline appeared to have stabilized, but it has left many, many Americans without close ties to any religious community. Research has shown that Americans often consult psychotherapists for problems that, fifty years ago, they would have taken to their minister, priest, or rabbi. So therapists are often confronting issues that in the past would have been labeled religious—ethical dilemmas regarding divorce or responsibilities to aging parents or growing children; vocational conflicts about switching jobs or even radically altering one's lifestyle; questions about personal meaning and the purpose of life. For these, and many other reasons, spirituality and psychology have been brought close together in many peoples' minds.

So it seemed natural for someone who has spent most of his professional life involved in trying to navigate the boundary between psychology and spirituality to write a book on that subject. Like all books, this book grew out of an author's life and work. Along with practicing as a psychologist, I have taught courses in religious studies for over thirty years—courses in world religions, philosophy of religion, and the place of religion in contemporary culture—and I have written books and articles on science and religion, religion in America, and religion and psychology. In addition, I am an ordained clergyman in the Episcopal Church and a sometime student of Tibetan Buddhism.

So this topic of the necessity of spiritual practice is here addressed by a professor of religion who is also a clinical psychologist. A clinical psychologist is a strange mixture of disciplines. I was trained at a school very committed to the so-called scientist-practitioner model of clinical psychology. The clinical psychologist was supposed to live and work continually on the interface between scientific research and human suffering. Like every psychologist, I learned how to design experiments, use statistics, review and critique the literature, keep current on the latest research reports, and all the other skills of a scientifically trained psychologist. These provided the solid scientific foundation on which clinical practice was to be erected.

Unlike the laboratory researcher, such technical skills as mastering threats to internal and external statistical validity, keeping within acceptable errors of measurement, ruthlessly criticizing others' designs and conclusions, and all the other practices of a well-trained psychologist, were necessary but not sufficient. The clinical psychologist must also learn to interview empathetically, keep detachment and compassion balanced in the face of the rage and pain of fellow human beings, translate knowledge gained in the antisepsis of the laboratory into interventions useful to teenagers on the verge of suicide or couples whose love has curdled into verbal (and sometimes physical) abuse. So the clinical psychologist lives on the boundary between social science and human suffering.

For me there was also the boundary between psychology and spirituality. There are many different ways of living on that boundary, too. The devout Christian who becomes a social psychologist and studies the role of values in human behavior. The rigorous Buddhist practitioner who uses mediation in her behavioral medicine practice. The person raised in a spiritualist tradition who becomes a Jungian analyst. The former fundamentalist who pursues the psychology of religion as part of his continuing war against his past.

For me the boundary between religion and psychology runs in a rather different direction. For me to speak psychologically about religion is to become conscious of what attracts us to the speculations of the Upanishads and the image of the drop of water vanishing into the sea; or to the koans of Zen Buddhism and the lure of emptiness; or to the heroics of Camus and Sartre; or to the stern demands of Allah; or to the wisdom of Torah; or to the soaring calculations of Einstein, whose God does not play dice; or to the grace of Jesus; or to the love of the Great Mother, who conjures power from the earth; or to the embracing universal archetypes of Jung. To speak psychologically about the spiritual life is to understand how the spiritual expressions we choose relate to the rest of our personal history. And I will try to do that here, about myself, in the coming chapters. So sections of this book have a frankly autobiographical cast.

Whenever I lecture about spirituality, psychology, and modern culture, people ask how I came to see these things in the idiosyncratic way that I do. They want to know how I came to stand with one foot in the camp of ancient spiritual practices like meditation, prayer, and the traditional Holy Communion liturgy, and the other foot in the camp of modern psychology, philosophy, and natural science. The autobiographical sections, dispersed throughout the book, represent my best attempt at an answer to that question.

In addition, if an author is going to discuss such deeply personal topics as those raised by religion and psychology and the dialogue between them, he owes the reader some idea of where he is coming from and what experiences and reflections stand behind the positions he takes. The personal experiences recounted throughout this book are part of the foundation for the discussions that follow in the coming chapters.

Furthermore, from a psychological standpoint, every spiritual practice, if it is personally authentic, must arise out of and take root in the individual's life and personality. Part of consciously choosing or recommitting yourself to a spiritual path as an adult is to examine your own life and understand how the disciplines to which you commit yourself fit with your personal history and your individual needs and wishes. Thus continual self-examination, whether it is the searching moral inventory called for by Alcoholics Anonymous or the ongoing process of spiritual direction common in the Christian and Buddhist traditions, is a part of the spiritual journey. For this reason, too, this book contains various autobiographical reflections.

Another obvious context in which this book is written, besides my individual life and work, is that of contemporary American culture. A spiritual practice undertaken today, in a culture deeply influenced by psychology and strongly committed to individualism, will be very different from one undertaken in medieval Europe or eighth-century Tibet or premodern Japan. This is true even if the practice is called Christian mysticism or Tantric Buddhism or Zen. Throughout this book I will be taking what I call "cultural interludes" in order to point out some of the places where various currents in our culture impact our spiritual practices.

Another context for this book is a growing interest in the possible relationships between Christianity and Buddhism. Every major city has at least one center devoted to programs on spiritual development. Catalogues from such places advertise many programs on Buddhist and Christian spiritualities, and some on both together. Spiritually focused magazines often run articles on Buddhism and Christianity in the same issue. One of the most influential voices in contemporary spirituality, the Catholic monk Thomas Merton, died while in Asia meeting with Buddhist leaders. From the other side, an influential contemporary Buddhist monk, Thich Nhat Hanh, has written books about Jesus from a Buddhist perspective (and an introduction to one of Merton's books). I know of several Catholic priests who have studied in Buddhist monasteries. At a more intellectual level, the last several decades have witnessed many conferences bringing Christian and Buddhist monastics together. At the more local level, I recently visited a spirituality center in a suburban community, which is headed by an Episcopal priest and run out of an Episcopal church that recently had a Tibetan lama give a series of lectures. I know of a local Zen meditation group headed by a Roman Catholic priest (who studied in a Zen monastery) meeting in another Episcopal church. It is not at all unusual to have active members of Protestant and Catholic parishes going to Buddhist meditation centers and incorporating some Buddhist practices into their Christian lives. And, of course, most people in America today who claim a Buddhist practice were not born Buddhists, but Christians or Jews.

Much of the discussion in this book uses comparisons between Christianity and Buddhism. Such comparisons draw upon this ongoing dialogue between Christianity and Buddhism in which I have also been engaged for many years. These conversations indicate that there are many Christians who are interested in knowing, not only about Buddhist beliefs and practices, but also more about Christianity's possible relationship to Buddhism and Buddhism's possible relationship to Christianity. Chapter three will explore some of the larger convergences and divergences between these two traditions.

The first chapter describes why it is better to approach Christianity as a spiritual practice rather than a set of beliefs or a moral code. The second chapter takes up the tricky question of what is meant by Christian spirituality. I think it is incumbent on anyone using a word that has acquired so many diverse (and sometimes contradictory) meanings to be clear to his readers about what he means by the word "spirituality," especially in a Christian context. I try to do that in chapter two.

Chapter four reviews the latest research on the relationship between religious practice and mental and physical health in order to demonstrate some of the positive effects of taking up a spiritual practice. Such research, while conducted within rigorous scientific standards, calls into question two of the fundamental assumptions of a secular technological society: that the only source of knowledge is the scientific method, and that human happiness can be achieved through material possessions alone. Spiritual practice is thus a potent form of cultural critique, directly questioning the principles by which many of us live our lives. Christian and Buddhist spiritual disciplines challenge many of the building blocks of modern society and provide alternative ways of experiencing ourselves and our relation to the world around us.

The fifth chapter lays out in some detail how I came to dwell on this boundary between psychotherapy and spirituality. It is frankly autobiographical. Those who are not interested in an author's personal story and how his work reflects his life can skip this chapter if they wish.

How do the benefits of spiritual discipline occur? How does spiritual practice really impact on our daily lives? Partly through transforming us and making us different people. This process of transformation, which I call becoming a spiritual self, is described in chapter six. This chapter tells how such spiritual selfhood enables us to live successfully and creatively in our everyday life.

Chapter seven explores in more detail exactly how spiritual disciplines increase our ability to handle life. But the story cannot end there. Spiritual discipline is more than just a coping strategy. It is also a means of personal and social transformation. The book concludes on that note—the centrality of an ongoing process of personal and social transformation.

CHAPTER ONE

Faith as Practice

Understanding requires doing.

I did not learn diagnosis from simply reading a textbook. God help you if you go to a doctor and her only training in diagnosis came from reading a text. To learn diagnosis, I had to take that textbook and its descriptions of psychological disorders out onto the floor of the hospital. I had to actually see patients and watch those more experienced than I making diagnoses.

If I want to really understand physics, I can't simply read a physics text. I have to spend time in a laboratory, performing experiments and drawing conclusions from them. If I want to learn an athletic skill or to play a musical instrument, I have to practice by doing it over and over again, under the watchful eye of an accomplished performer. Medical diagnosis, physics, musical instruments, martial arts are learned primarily by apprenticeship, by practicing them under the direction of someone with experience.

You cannot become a psychotherapist just from reading books. Therapy is learned by spending years doing it under supervision. And when you want to learn a new way of doing therapy, then you have to start over with new supervision. When I wanted to learn hypnosis, for example, I not only took several classes in using hypnosis and read many books. I also went to workshops where the techniques were practiced under supervision and spent two years doing hypnosis under the direction of an experienced practitioner even though I had been doing other kinds of psychotherapy for several years.

We can distinguish two kinds of knowledge. I can have a "secondhand knowledge" from reading a book. Many years ago I was writing a book on science and religion and as part of that project I needed to learn something about physics. So I sat in on a few classes, read some books for the layperson, and got some tutoring from a colleague in the physics department. I got to the point where I could comprehend some articles in some journals, if they weren't too mathematical, and understand some of the visiting lecturers. But this certainly did not make me a physicist. In order to actually become a physicist, I would have had to spend long hours working in the laboratory or at the computer. That is, I would have had to learn to practice the discipline called physics.

This is also true of Christianity. And every religion. I can go to my local bookstore and buy books from the religion section, maybe take a course in Religion at the university. This will enable me to understand the definitions of some major terms and to go to a lecture and listen to it with understanding. But that does not make me a Christian. Or a Buddhist. I do not see the world or face life as a Christian or a Buddhist does from reading books or hearing lectures. To do that, I have to undertake the practices that make up the spiritual life in Christianity or Buddhism. Such discipline is essential in religion and in science.

Beliefs and Practices

A major problem in modern culture is that we separate theory from practice. In our educational system and mass media, we often focus on abstract ideas and not on the practices from which they emerge. Nowhere has that done more mischief than in the study of religion. Often, if I ask university students what comes into their minds when they hear the word "religion," they immediately think of creeds and beliefs. Ideas. But these ideas and beliefs often seem abstract to my students because these concepts have been removed from the context of practice in which they make sense.

Words only make sense in a context of practice. If I pick up a book about nuclear physics and have never studied physics, I may stumble over terms like "elementary particle" or "wave function." These terms make no sense outside the field of physics. I can look up an abstract definition in the glossary at the end of the textbook, but I don't really know what these terms mean unless I know what the physicist *does* with them: how they help her make sense of an experiment or design a new research project. At a party I may overhear a psychologist using terms like "reinforcement theory" or "contingency contracts." To really understand them, I would have to know how the psychologist *uses* them to explain why a child's behavior is out of control or to help a person recovering from a stroke regain some of their lost abilities. Separating theory and practice has turned many words into abstractions. To counter that, we must return our words to their connection to our lived experience. Disciplined practice is the way that connection is made.

Christianity is not an abstract theory. The beliefs of Christianity only make sense in the midst of the struggle to love God with our heart and mind and soul and to love our neighbor as ourselves. Terms like God, prayer, redemption can only be understood if I know how the Christian uses them to make sense of his experience, to live a life of compassion and justice, to deepen her awareness of God. If I want a firsthand understanding of the Christian life, I have to live the Christian life. If I want a deeper spiritual experience, I must undertake a deeper spiritual practice.

In science and religion, as well as in art, medicine, and psychology, words only make sense in a context of practice. The meaning of a term is best understood by seeing the use to which it is put. The languages of (for example) physics, Christianity, and clinical psychology are designed to enable the practitioners of those disciplines to do things they want to do: to create experiments, live a spiritually oriented life, treat emotional disorders. The concepts found in physics, psychology, Christianity, and Buddhism enable people to engage in and understand these practices—practices to which they have devoted their lives.

There is a circle here between belief and practice, each influencing the other. The beliefs of (again), say, physics, Christianity, and clinical psychology help their practitioners understand experiences they encounter along the way. The theories of physics help physicists interpret the results of a just-completed experiment. The teachings of Christianity help Christians make sense of their awareness of the presence of God. The ideas found in clinical psychology textbooks help psychotherapists figure out the connection between a patient's interpersonal history and his depression. Here, too, practice plays a crucial role. The *practice* of physics or Christian spirituality or clinical psychology gives rise to these experiences that I am trying to understand within these fields. Running experiments generates the data the physicist has to interpret. Spending time in prayer and meditation and devotional reading sets a context in which the presence of God is encountered. Taking a careful personal history generates the information about the patient that the therapist has to work with. In all these examples, the practices of the field give rise to certain experiences *and* the theories, teachings, and beliefs found in that field provide categories by which these experiences can be understood and guide the practitioners in developing new practices and formulating new theories. Practices generate new experiences and provide the categories in which these experiences are understood: this circle characterizes every vital human activity.

Part of learning a new discipline is learning to experience things in a particular way. A biology student might say to me, "Dr. Jones, come to my laboratory and look through the microscope and you will see mitochondria." Not a chance! If I look through that microscope, I will see only what William James called a "blooming, buzzing, confusion." But if I study biology, then I will be able to see the deeper structures of cellular life. Or I might take an art student over to the physics laboratory and show him a photograph of a high-energy experiment—a black and white tracing of intricate lines and swirls, the tracks of elementary particles colliding. The art student might say, "What a beautiful work, I would like to frame it and hang it on my wall." Of course the trained physicist sees there the fundamental structures of the material universe. If you study medicine, what before seemed like disconnected swellings and pains now appear as symptoms of an infection. Part of learning a new discipline is learning to see new things: the structures of the cell, the traces of elementary particles, the presence of disease.

Likewise with Christianity. And any religion. Undertaking a spiritual discipline involves learning to experience things in a new way. A book formerly regarded as an out-of-date historical document now becomes a guide to contemporary life. Events previously dismissed as meaningless coincidences are now seen as graciously meaningful. An unexpected tragedy now becomes an opportunity to meditate on the transitory nature of life. Periods of meditation yield previously undreamed-of insights into the deepest Source of our life. As with physics, medicine, and clinical psychology, in Christianity too, practices shape what we experience. Practicing a science, a clinical art, or a religion is (among other things) training oneself to experience the world in a different way.

Beliefs and practices are not antagonists. Undertaking a practice depends upon certain fundamental beliefs and commitments. I would not begin the arduous study of physics unless I believed it would be fruitful and productive of new knowledge and be personally satisfying. I would not commit myself to the many years of training to become a clinical psychologist without the faith that it would help suffering people and expand my understanding of human behavior. The faith required to undertake such studies as physics or psychology is not blind faith. Teachers and supervisors and revered researchers have undertaken these journeys before me. Their examples inspire me and show that such fundamental beliefs and commitments can be intellectually and socially fruitful and personally satisfying, and that such faith is not misplaced. But I will not know that for myself unless I make the commitments, accept the beliefs, and learn the practices.

I cannot prove that to the skeptic. The convictions and commitments basic to a science or an art cannot be proven in advance. I can point to examples but I cannot logically demonstrate that scientific study will be fruitful, that order and regularity can be discovered in new domains of nature, that running or mountain-climbing can be exhilarating, or that living a socially connected life is better than a life of bitterness and isolation. Such truths can only be known (in a "firsthand" sense) by those willing to commit themselves to them. The contemporary philosopher of science Michael Polanyi says that basic truths are those things that are only "proven true" by those willing to stake their lives (or part of their lives) on them and live them out.

Obviously the same thing is true with Christianity. And any religion. The practices of Christianity or Buddhism depend upon certain basic beliefs and commitments: that meditation, worship, devotional reading, and moral action will lead me to new truths, transform me into the kind of moral person

I want to become, and be personally fulfilling. Again I cannot prove in advance to the skeptic that meditation can deepen the sense of divine presence, that devotional reading can produce new insights, that communal worship can strengthen moral commitments, that sitting Zazen ("sitting meditation") will produce enlightenment, or that it is more blessed to give than to receive. Like the basic beliefs of the natural sciences or the clinical arts, these basic convictions are only "proven true" by living them out. Like the basic beliefs of the natural sciences and the clinical arts, the basic beliefs of a religion are known to be true by their potential to make sense of the very experiences that these same commitments and practices make available—be they the data of carefully contrived experiments in the case of natural science, or the diagnoses of carefully observed patients in the case of medicine and psychology, or the enlightenments gained through disciplined meditation in the case of Christianity and Buddhism.

Of course the beliefs and commitments involved in undertaking the practices associated with Christianity or Buddhism may appear more like blind faith than those associated with physics, medicine, or psychology. This is because, in our contemporary popular culture, many fewer people have undertaken the disciplined spiritual journey. And so many fewer examples are available to encourage us and serve as demonstrations of the fruitfulness of such a life. Nobel Prize–winning scientists and breakthrough medical researchers are prominently featured in the media (as well they should be). They are the cultural heroes of a technological society even when the actual science behind their discoveries is poorly understood. But often in the popular media, religious figures are only featured when they have done serious mischief: coerced young people into cultish dependence, seduced their devotees, absconded with the collection, or been found in bed with a prostitute. Thus the commitment to undertake the spiritual journey may feel to us today much more like blind faith or a dead end than undertaking the journeys of discovery at the heart of physics or medicine. But this is simply a matter of cultural relativity. We live in a society that provides few models and examples of the fruitfulness of the spiritual life. So anyone undertaking this journey is apt to feel alone and marginal. But without such a disciplined journey, there is no firsthand knowledge of religious truth.

Spiritual Practice in Early Christianity

I know this is a very controversial claim: that Christianity should be more centered on practice and experience than on belief. For much of its history Western Christianity has been centered around having the correct belief. The criteria for whether one is, or is not, a Christian have usually involved accepting certain dogmas or believing certain claims, such as "Jesus is the Messiah." Much religious energy from the medieval philosophers through the reformation theologians to contemporary religious thinkers has been expended on defining, clarifying, and often defending the correct set of beliefs.

But there is another stream of Christianity, neglected in the modern world, which does not focus primarily on belief. This tradition, going back to the earliest theologians of the Christian Church, attends more to religious practices, and the experiences of oneself and God that arise from them, than to beliefs.

Recently I have been reading some of these very early Christian writers on spirituality—from the first few Christian centuries—and one of the things that struck me was how psychological in a certain sense they were. They make the site of redemption the individual's interior struggle with themselves. They provide meditation techniques to help quiet the mind. For example, the Christian seeker is told to repeat the "Jesus Prayer" ("Lord Jesus Christ, have mercy upon me") in time with her breathing and the beating of her heart. The "heart" in these texts refers not only to the physical organ or to the seat of emotions, but also to a part of ourselves that is deeper than our thoughts and feelings. For these early Christian writers, the "heart" is our spiritual center, the "image of God" within us, the interior sanctuary wherein the meeting of the self and its divine source is consummated. Through such a practice as repeating the phrase "Lord Jesus Christ, have mercy upon me," this "Jesus Prayer" is said to "take up residence" in the heart, that is, in the center of our life. These spiritual masters often call this practice "a prayer of the heart," which means a prayer of the whole person, encompassing our thoughts and feelings and even our bodies.

One goal of such practices is called "watchfulness," which might be translated as attentiveness or alertness. Buddhists call it "mindfulness." It means entering the interior place of tranquility. Watchfulness "is the heart's still-ness . . . free from mental images . . . unbroken by any thought," as one early Christian teacher put it. Here we become aware of something about ourselves that we cannot learn in any other way—that there is a place of peacefulness within.

Another goal of these practices is to connect us to the divine source of our life through the recitation of the name of Jesus. You can think of this recitation as either implanting that connection within us or as awakening a connection that is already latent there. In Christian belief, Jesus represents the meeting place of the human and the divine. That is the meaning of the Church's creedal statement that Jesus is both "fully God and fully human." By focusing and refocusing our attention on this image of human-divine connection represented in the stories of Jesus' life, ministry, death, and res-urrection, we reestablish that connection within our consciousness. As the Gospel of John says, "to all who received him, who believed in his name [which this tradition takes as a reference to the Jesus Prayer], he gave power to become children of God; who were born not of blood, nor of the will of the flesh, nor of the will of man, but of God" (1:12–13).

Through the prayer of the heart we, too, like him, become born of God. Or as the second-century theologian Irenaeus put it, "he became like us that we might become like him." By synchronizing the Jesus Prayer to our breathing and heartbeat, early Christian teachers claimed that the divine presence comes to reside in out heart (that is, in the center of our self)."In this stillness the heart breathes and invokes [the Jesus Prayer], endlessly and without ceasing" is how one early Christian writer put it. Statements like "Jesus is the Messiah" or the doctrine of the Trinity are not primarily intel-lectual concepts to be believed or disbelieved. Rather they are objects of con-templation that can evoke new insights and personal transformations if meditated on. I will return to this point in the next chapter.

Concentrating on the movement of one's breath in and out of one's body is a venerable technique in virtually every religious tradition. It is central in Theravada Buddhist "mindfulness meditation" and the zazen of Zen Bud-dhism. Hindus practicing mantra meditation utilize the breath as do Chris-tians praying the Jesus Prayer. Reflecting on the constancy of the breath evokes for us the constancy of that spiritual source that maintains and sustains us in this life and throughout eternity. Allowing ourselves to relax into that experience of being sustained can open up an interior space of great stillness and calm.

Recent laboratory research has demonstrated some of the physiological benefits of such a practice. This research was pioneered by Herbert Benson, who called the physical effect of this practice the "relaxation response." Among the demonstrated health benefits that flow from sustained attention to your breathing include lowering blood pressure and heart rate, reducing chronic pain, lowering blood cholesterol levels, and improvement in many chronic and acute illnesses. In addition it also affects our brain waves, reduces central nervous system reactivity, lowers anxiety, and is associated with improvements in mood and well-being.

Repeating the phrase "Lord Jesus Christ, have mercy upon me," or any short, spiritually significant phrase in time to our breathing will evoke that interior stillness and quiet. However, any meditator, regardless of tradition, knows that in this stillness all the thoughts that arise are far from holy or prayerful. If we try to simply keep our attention fixed on the movement of our breathing, we will soon find our minds wondering far afield. Our leg feels cramped. We remember the phone call we forgot to make. We get a sudden insight we can't help but mull over. And so it goes.

Given the universal reality of such distractions, this early Christian tradition also provided psychological suggestions for working with these distracting thoughts and memories as well as with the bodily sensations like hunger or sexual fantasy that arise in the course of meditation. In the midst of this stillness, the spiritual practitioner is taught to watch closely the movements of his or her desire so as to develop the capacity for detached observation and careful discrimination of her wishes and desires. Through techniques such as concentrated breathing, extensive visualizing of episodes from the life of Christ, reciting the Jesus Prayer, human desire is not to be suppressed but refocused. The purpose of these practices was an ever-deepening and more accurate knowledge of our motivations, strengths, and weaknesses and enough self-discipline to direct our energies toward "doing justice, loving mercy, and walking humbly with God." Today we think that expanding our awareness, gaining insight into our motivations, changing our patterns of thought and behavior are the task of psychology. In the first centuries of the Christian faith, these were the goals of spiritual practice.

Spiritual Practice In Buddhism and Christianity

This practice of repeating a spiritually powerful phrase is not unique to early Christianity. Very similar practices have existed for thousands of years within Tibetan Buddhism (and other schools of Buddhism) and Hinduism, where they are often called "mantras" or "mantra vehicles" (that is reciting a mantra as a vehicle to get us to enlightenment). The term "mantra" comes from a Sanskrit word that means "tool for the mind"—a tool the mind uses to calm and focus itself and incorporate a spiritual reality (for a Christian, the presence of Christ or the connection to God) within oneself. Whereas these early Christians relied almost exclusively on the Jesus Prayer as a tool to center their minds, the Tibetan Buddhists developed an extensive repertoire of different mantras for different purposes. There are Tibetan mantras to develop compassion, to heal the body, to gain new insights into the nature of reality. While also emphasizing the meaning of a mantra in focusing the mind on a certain spiritual truth (for example, the compassion of the Buddha or a revered Buddhist saint), the Tibetans also attend to the actual, physical power of the sounds of the words of the mantra. Some of their mantras have very little meaning for the mind to attend to. Instead their power is said to derive from the ability of the sound itself to awaken various unconscious aspects of the human spirit.

In addition, in Pure Land Buddhism mantras are often chanted. There is a chant that translates approximately "Praise to Amida Buddha." And in Nicherin Buddhism chanting the mantra "Praise to the Lotus Sutra" is a major spiritual practice.

Of course there are other types of Buddhist meditation besides those using a mantra or spiritual phrase. Theravada Buddhism (the most prevalent Buddhism in Southeast Asia) and Zen have meditational techniques that involve focusing primarily on the bare cycle of breathing. This "mindfulness meditation" follows the simple rule (simple to state, not simple to do) that we described earlier and that has parallels in the writings of the early Christian masters referred to before: attend to your breathing and simply observe whatever thoughts, feelings, or memories pass through your awareness and, when you realize you have been distracted by some fleeting thought, gently return your awareness to your breath. Practiced over and over, this deceptively simple technique will gradually develop that "observing self" that can watch the sensations of consciousness without becoming involved with them. And since all experience comes to us as sensations in our minds, as we become more detached from those sensations, we develop the Buddhist virtue of nonattachment. This nonattachment is the goal of mindfulness meditation.

My favorite illustration of the heart of Buddhism—nonattachment—is the Zen Buddhist story about the abbot of a monastery in Japan. Soldiers attacked the monastery and all the monks fled. When the leader of the invading army broke into the inner courtyard of the monastery, he found the abbot standing tall in the middle. "Why haven't you fled? Don't you know who I am?" the soldier demanded. "I could run you through with my sword and not blink an eye." "Don't you know who I am?" the abbot replied. "I could watch you run me through with your sword and not blink an eye."

Buddhism is not content to simply teach about such nonattachment. Buddhism offers techniques designed to produce it. The main such technique is this mindfulness meditation. The Buddhist ideal of mindfulness or nonattached observation that brings tranquility in its wake is very similar to the early Christian ideal of watchfulness.

I think it is unlikely that contemporary Christians can follow Tibetan Buddhists and understand the power of meditative phrases to reside in their sounds. But there is no reason why Christians cannot adopt a variety of different meditative techniques for different purposes. For example, for spiritual development I prefer something like the Jesus Prayer. My mind is just too wandering and I need a concrete phrase on which to focus. But when I primarily want the psychological and physical effects of meditation, like relaxation, I prefer to simply concentrate on my breathing. And I don't only use the classical Jesus Prayer. I often use instead the ancient single-word Aramaic Christian prayer "maranatha"—meaning "Come Lord Jesus"—or a phrase from the Lord's Prayer.

The Role of the Body

By concentrating on breathing and heartbeat as part of meditation, both the early Christian writers and the Tibetan teachers are calling attention to the crucial role of the body in spiritual practice. The early Christian writers seem much more ambivalent about the body than do the Tibetan Buddhists. They speak of the importance of attending to the breath and heartbeat and working with drives like hunger and lust as a part of Christian practice. But they clearly subscribed to the extreme body-soul dualism prevalent in their culture, in which spirit and body were seen as antagonists. So the body usually appears in their writings as a hindrance to spiritual growth and as something to be tamed and controlled through spiritual discipline. Such a negative view of the body has persisted throughout Christian history. This view of the body as necessarily opposed to the spiritual life ignores that we are told in the Book of Genesis that God looked upon the physical creation and declared it "good." Such an antiphysical viewpoint also deprives Christians of practices that can further spiritual development through disciplines that work directly with the body.

Here, I think, the Buddhists have something to teach Christianity. Rather than seeing the body as an antagonist to the spirit, Tibetan and Zen Buddhists approach the body in a much more nuanced way. Of course they would agree with the early Christians that uncontrolled anger or rampant lust are impediments to spiritual development. But for them the body itself is as much an expression of the spirit as an enemy of it. In Buddhism the physical body is only one dimension of embodied life. There are also bodily realities that are nonphysical.

This is almost impossible for contemporary Westerners to grasp. We are used to understanding the body exclusively in terms of the categories of physical science. Western Christians may also believe in a nonphysical, nonbodily soul lying beyond the purview of science. The rise of natural science in the modern period has simultaneously intensified the heritage of mind-body dualism that goes back to the earliest days of the Church and has undermined it. By making the body purely a part of the physical world, controlled by mechanical laws, science has made the body seem even more irrelevant to the spiritual life. And by reducing all human experience to physical forces, science has seemed to undermine the possibility of any spiritual reality within human nature. So, given the antibody heritage of Christianity and the hegemony of the scientific worldview, these seem to many contemporary Christians like the only possible alternatives: a purely material body as described by natural science, and (perhaps) a nonphysical soul loosely connected (if at all) to the purely physical body. The idea of bodily realities that are not physical can find no place in such a schema.

In Tibetan Buddhism, alongside the muscles and neurons described by the biological sciences exists an intricate series of what the Tibetans call "winds." There is no precise word in English with which to translate this term. It is usually referred to as a "subtle energy": "energy" in the sense of a force or power that can affect the body and "subtle" in the sense of nonphysical. These winds move through the body by means of a complex network of channels, 72,000 in all. The major channel is the spinal column, along which are a series of eight connection points called "wheels" (or "chakras"). Consciousness is said to "ride upon the winds" and so move through the body, directing the flow of subtle energy. The physical body is but the most solid expression of this complex of forces. One of the goals of Tibetan Buddhist meditation is to learn to control these winds and so direct consciousness into higher and more spiritual channels, thereby opening up new, more spiritual realms of conscious experience. Traditional Tibetan practitioners appear to experience their bodies less as physical machines and more as complex systems of physiological-spiritual forces over which the meditator can, after years of practice, gain a certain amount of conscious control. For them the body is less an impediment to, and more a vehicle for, spiritual growth.

Zen Buddhist physiology is simpler than Tibetan. Instead of the eight chakras, there are three centers ("tanden" in Japanese, "dantian" in Chinese) located along the spine—one at the base of the spine, one near the solar plexus, and one at the forehead. Instead of the thousands of channels, there is a compact series of "meridians" along which flows a single force called "ki" in Japanese or "chi" in Chinese. Here too the physical body is an extension of this nonphysical but bodily power. The physical body is a carrier of this force that is, in a healthy body, in continual circulation.

This force is not restricted to the human body, however. It is also circulating through the physical universe. In traditional Chinese philosophy, this subtle power, which gives rise to the physical world, was called the "Tao," which is the "source of creation" that "overflows and spreads on every side! All being comes from it, no creature is denied." Such is the Tao. Whereas Western science segregates the body from the rest of the physical world and treats the body as a self-contained mechanism of parts and forces, Buddhism sees the psycho-physical person as an open system in continual, mutual interaction with the rest of the universe—a mutual interaction going on at both the purely physical level through the exchange of oxygen, food, and activity, and also at the more subtle level of the chi forces moving through the world.

Tibetan Buddhism tends to approach the task of working with this nonphysical but bodily energy primarily through the training of consciousness by means of meditative and visualization disciplines of exquisite subtlety. There are physical practices in Tibetan Buddhism as well: breathing techniques, elaborate prostrations before the statues of the Buddha, and rarely (if ever) used procedures involving the transformation of sexual desire. But most attention is given to mantra recitation, chanting, and visualizing images of Buddhist deities and teachers in the finest detail possible in order to restructure our ways of experiencing ourselves and our bodies and the world.

While centering their practice on sitting meditation, Zen Buddhism also draws on its psycho-spiritual physiology in developing a series of physical activities that work directly with the body and its chi. The most well-known of these physio-spiritual practices are the various schools of Chinese and Japanese martial arts such as Tai-Chi, Kung Fu, Aikido, and Karate.

In keeping with the preoccupations of American culture, in the United States these arts have been turned into competitive sports. In their traditional settings they were only one part of a more encompassing system of spiritual development that also included meditation practice, study, and ethical behavior. All of these disciplines were designed to work together to transform the person in accordance with Buddhist ideals. The physical practices of the martial arts and the meditational exercises that accompanied them were designed to both connect the individual to the subtle, nonphysical energy circulating in the universe and to activate and transform that chi-force within the individual into a higher or more spiritual form, thereby (as in Tibetan Buddhism) opening up new, more spiritual realms of conscious experience.

This is often described in the literature as a process of raising the chi from the lower dantian at the base of the spine, which is associated with sexual energy, to the top dantian at the forehead, associated with spiritual experiences of oneness with the universe and insight into the true nature of reality. This process is carried out through various meditation and visualization practices that include visualizing the chi as a liquid or a flame or a dragon rising up from the base (lower dantian) through the spine and finally arriving at the top of the forehead. In Buddhism sexuality and spirituality (the lower and higher dantian) are not antagonists but rather arise as different permutations of the same system of energy, and the body is experienced as a vehicle for spiritual development.

Such a view may seem foreign to Christianity. However, the Gospel of John begins with the claim that "In the beginning ['arche' in Greek, which also means origin or source] was the Word ['Logos' in Greek], and the Word was with God, and the Word was God. He was in the beginning with God; all things were made through him, and without him nothing was made. In him was life and the life was the light of men" (1: 1–4). The Greek term "Logos" does not mean "word" in our ordinary English sense. Logos is not a part of speech. Logos was a common philosophical concept in the first century. It referred to the deepest structure of the universe, more fundamental than anything studied by physicists then or now. The Logos was the creative and ordering principle of the universe, giving rise to the laws and patterns that science discovers. The orderliness of nature, the elegance of mathematics, the beauty found in art and music, the complexity of the human mind, are all expressions of the Logos. The Gospel of John is affirming that the original source and sustaining power of the universe is the Logos energy that is revealed in the life and work of Jesus of Nazareth.

The Logos was not a philosophical abstraction. It was more like a living soul or spirit: a lively and energetic force existing throughout the physical cosmos, forming and guiding all events. In many philosophical schools at the time of Jesus and the Apostles (especially Stoicism), the Logos was referred to as a world soul of which it could be said, "in him was life and the life was the light of humankind." The wise man or woman lived in harmony with the Logos. The Logos provided a deep and fundamental continuity throughout the system of nature, stretching from the most elementary particles to the most complex neurological systems—all were manifestations and variations on the omnipresent Logos.

The idea of a pervasive, vital, nonphysical force existing throughout the universe including the human organism and revealed in Jesus of Nazareth is found throughout the New Testament. This image is implicit in the opening chapter of the Gospel of John, which speaks of one "through whom all things were made . . . a light that enlightens everyone." Paul also speaks this way when he writes in his Letter to the Colossians that Christ is "the image of the invisible God, the first born of all creation; for in him all things were created . . . all things were created through him and for him. He existed before all things and in him all things are held together. . . . He is the origin." Here the Christ, the Logos, is the cosmic glue that holds the physical universe together. He is the origin—again, "arche" in Greek, the same philosophical term that occurs in the opening sentence of the Gospel of John and means the creative source of everything and the basis of the universe's coherence and unity. And the Letter to the Ephesians describes the plan of God revealed in Christ as, "when the time was ready the entire cosmos—things in heaven and things on earth—will be united together in Christ . . . the fullness of him who fills the entire universe." Jesus of Nazareth is, for the Christian, the manifestation of a subtle energy that pervades and powers the entire universe.

The universe has the form it does because of the presence of the Christ, the Logos, within it—the primal and immaterial spring from which the material world in all its variegations arises. The second-century Christian theologian Justin the Martyr also identified the Christ with the Logos and spoke of the Logos as "the seeds of truth sown throughout the world." The image here is of an immaterial spiritual source of the material world. Physical reality is the outward expression of spirit, or spirit is the interior ground of matter. The Logos is the Tao of Christianity.

I was well into my fifties when I started to train in Japanese Karate. Obviously at that age I had no illusions about becoming a competitive martial artist. And many acquaintances thought it an odd thing to do at that point in my life. At first it was mostly for the physical workout and the self-discipline. In keeping with my rather intellectual nature, I also began to buy and read books on the philosophy of the martial arts and their connection to Buddhist practice. There was no way I could learn the actual practice of Karate from reading a book. Like any discipline, it can only be learned by repetition under the direction of a skilled instructor. But from reading, I could learn about the philosophical and meditative dimensions of these arts.

Currently I need the physical workout more than ever. And I certainly appreciate the confidence in regards to self-defense that I have gained. Recently my daughter asked me if I thought I could defend myself. I replied I certainly thought so but I would do anything to keep from having to. But there is nothing like breaking a few boards with a punch or throwing to the ground a bigger man charging me with a club or knife to give me a certain confidence. I continue to train several times a week. But along with the physical training, I have been trying to incorporate into my own spiritual practice some of the meditative exercises associated with the martial arts, designed to work with the body's subtle energies.

Without going into too much detail about my own practices, I can say that I try to build upon the more basic meditational discipline of concentrating on the cycle of breathing and, at least for me, repeating the Jesus Prayer or some other Christian mantra. Then, drawing on the Logos imagery in Paul and John, I may visualize myself as part of this encompassing system of subtle energies called the cosmos and to experience those energies circulating through me. Often this is accompanied by a tingling sensation, reminiscent of the experience of accidentally touching a live electrical outlet. Sometimes I focus my attention on that spot at the base of my spine where the energy of the Tao or Logos is said to be concentrated.

This embodied dimension of spiritual practice, while hinted at in the early Christian writers' attention to breath and heartbeat during meditation, has been underdeveloped in Christianity. Without having to train in Tai-Chi or Karate, Christians might learn something of the role of the body by incorporating into their religious discipline some of the body-based meditative practices from Buddhism. They might also learn something of the body's subtle, spiritual powers and its intimate connection with the rest of the universe. Such ideas may well be latent in the Logos-theology of the Gospel of John.

In arguing for the primacy of practice, I am not saying that beliefs are irrelevant. But I am suggesting they are secondary, derived from experience and useful to the extent that they make sense of the experiences we are having, experiences born from practices like contemplation, ritual participation, a meditative reading of sacred books.

The Problem of Pluralism

Here we must take a cultural interlude and look at how this advocacy of spiritual practice interfaces with our contemporary culture. As we all know, we live in a pluralistic world and there is a pluralistic style of spiritual-seeking happening today that feels free simply to explore several different religious traditions at once. There are several reasons for this spiritual eclecticism.

One reason is because the mass media have created one world spiritually. You can go into your local bookstore and buy the sacred texts of religious traditions that your grandparents didn't even know existed. These ancient texts from around the globe can be found in colorful, easy to read English translations. A fragment from the ancient Palestinian Essenes and their "Dead Sea scrolls," an account of a formerly secret Tibetan meditation discipline, a manual of Sufi practice, the Kabbala (traditionally available only in Hebrew and to those over a certain age), and on and on it goes for shelf after shelf. You can take them home, light a candle, meditate on them, and see what happens.

Or, in any medium-size city you can probably find a center that caters to spiritual seekers. There you can meet respectable gurus from India, lamas from Tibet, masters from Japan and China, Buddhist and Christian monks in dialogue with Jewish rabbis—a long, winding multicultural parade. Television documentaries, speedy air travel, mass marketing of books on every conceivable tradition, university courses on world religions have all made us aware of the existence of other traditions in ways our ancestors never were. Information on a variety of religions is now more widely available and accessible than at any other time in human history. Any informed spiritual seeker today must find ways to take account of the full range of human spiritual traditions and teachings.

Another reason for this pluralistic style of spirituality involves the age cohort that came into prominence in the eighties and nineties—the so-called baby-boom generation. One oft-commented on characteristic of this group is its suspicion of institutions, nurtured by coming of age during the Watergate scandal, the government's massaging of the truth about what was happening in Vietnam, and the assassinations of revered political leaders (like the Kennedy brothers, and Martin Luther King, Jr.). Given this anti-institutionalism, it was natural that when members of this cohort went on a spiritual search, it would be outside the boundaries of traditional institutions.

A third reason for this eclectic style of spirituality, I think, involves the failure of major religious traditions creatively to come to terms with each other's existence. Many religious spokespersons appear to deny that other traditions exist or simply demand acceptance that their way is the one and only way without showing any real knowledge of the strengths of other traditions or the areas of weakness and failure in their own. Such arrogance, especially when backed by threats of force and other intimidations, ill becomes the cause of spiritual maturity. The failure of the major traditions to provide wisdom for those confronting the reality of religious pluralism is another reason why the spiritual search today often takes the form of sampling from the multicultural spiritual cafeteria of modern life.

This raises an important question that is beyond our scope in this book—What happens when you take a traditional practice out of its original context? Is it still the same? How is it changed? These are important questions, but they are not our focus here. Rather I simply want to underscore that this mighty pluralism makes it possible to sample spiritual disciplines from around the world. Any discussion of spiritual practice today must take this reality into account.

Speaking for myself, I think there is a gain to this pluralism and a possible problem.

On the positive side, this pluralism makes it possible (perhaps even necessary) to come to terms with each other's existence spiritually. This is a genuinely new, modern phenomena. For virtually the first time in human history, representatives of the world's religions are facing each other across tables and not just battlefields. And, more significantly, this is happening to ordinary Christian and Muslim and Buddhist believers, not only to priests and scholars and monks and other religious leaders.

This can be enriching. I have already written about how my Christian understanding of the role of the body in spiritual practice has been expanded by my training in Japanese martial arts and accompanying Buddhist meditational techniques. A later chapter will describe how my thinking about the Christian doctrine of the Trinity was stimulated by texts and discussions with Tibetan Buddhists. I know many Christians who have deepened their spiritual life by incorporating Zen Buddhist meditation into it. And Ghandi has written about how his Hindu ethical reflection was expanded by his encounter with the Jewish prophetic tradition while he was a student in England. Thus pluralism can be enriching.

But there is also a potential problem. There are some things we can only understand if we go deeply into them. Athletic skills, musical proficiency, theoretical physics, for example, are only gained by concentrated practice. If we try Zen meditation for a time, then take up the Jesus Prayer for a few months, and then try an Ignatian thirty-day retreat, we will certainly gain a lot. But there are riches in each practice that we will never tap.

The main point of many meditational disciplines—Christian centering prayer, Eastern Orthodoxy's Jesus Prayer, Japanese zazen, for example—is to develop and refine concentration. Too much shifting from practice to practice may undermine that goal.

Bill was a real spiritual seeker and his story illustrates this problem. After graduating from college in 1975, he went to India with a guru he had meet through a yoga society while in college. He stayed in the ashram for a year learning yoga until he became deathly ill and had to return home to Connecticut. He was in the hospital in a delirium for several weeks and at home recuperating for almost a year.

Then he moved to California and eventually lived in a Zen Buddhist monastery for one year. But having met a young woman who was a frequent retreatent there, he found himself unable to keep his vow of celibacy. He left that community and moved in with his girlfriend. They immediately got involved in a human potential group that featured very aggressive and punishing experiences including being yelled at by the leaders, forced to share intimate details of their lives, and kept from using the lavatory or eating for long periods of time. Bill worked part-time in a bookstore but all his energy went into this group until he came home one afternoon and found a note from his girlfriend saying she had moved in with one of the group's leaders. He immediately stopped attending but for months afterward was hounded by phone calls and people coming to his door demanding money they said he owed the group for the "training" he had received.

Bill then moved to Oregon and lived in a commune presided over by an Indian guru. He thrived in the group's routine of pre-dawn meditation followed by work on the farm and in the office followed by evening lectures and mediation. The group disbanded when the guru was forced to flee back to India after reports of sexual and financial misconduct brought the group to the notice of local authorities.

Bill moved back home again, went to graduate school, and obtained a degree in counseling and guidance and a job at a residential program for schizophrenic adolescents. He became a regular attendee at a center in New York City that sponsored a smorgasbord of workshops on meditation, body work, astrology, psychic abilities, and relationship problems. Clearly looking for something, he spent most of his young adulthood not finding it. He finally burned out of the spiritual search and in his thirties ceased all these activities. He got married, worked hard at his job and became director of guidance for a corporation that ran several psychiatric hospitals for adolescents. At forty he became depressed and sought treatment from me.

In his early forties, he still felt something spiritual was missing from his life. His attempts to articulate it were a jumble of terms and images from the history of religions: he spoke of cosmic energy, the universal Buddha nature, of raising the "Kundalini" (a Hindu term for the bodily energy), of getting "clear," of working with the body, of achieving "satori" (a Zen term for enlightenment). And on and on. But he could never really communicate clearly (even to me, someone familiar with world religions and sympathetic to the spiritual journey) what these terms meant to him or what he felt was lacking. None of the traditions and practices he had sampled had provided him with the language in which to articulate his deepest desires or the discipline to go deeply enough within either himself or a tradition to strike something lasting or solid. His moving from worldview to worldview was not a process of spiritual growth that could add up to a larger and more encompassing vision. It was rather a series of lateral movements that seemed to lead him nowhere. For all the time and effort he put into it, at midlife his spiritual searching had given him nothing substantive enough to commit himself to or to support and sustain his life.

Bill's story always seemed a parable to me of the pitfalls of shifting too quickly and easily from one spiritual practice to another. Knowledge requires doing, and that demands discipline. Any practice that enables us to learn, to experience, to see something new involves concentration. This is a wonderful time to be experimenting with adopting a spiritual practice. So much is available. But this richness can also create problems if it is not handled wisely.

I think that there is a significant difference between those, like my patient Bill, who jump from tradition to tradition and practice to practice, each time leaving behind most of what they've done before, and others, who temporarily move into a new tradition from a solid base in their own tradition, all the while remaining connected to their own tradition. Often those (like Bill) who have few roots in any tradition and simply flit from tradition to tradition fall short of a lasting and coherent spiritual practice. On the other hand, someone who is rooted in one tradition and who crosses over and engages in the practices of another tradition can enrich their own tradition and gain a deeper understanding of another's path. Such a person has a core tradition into which they can integrate their new learning and new practices, a foundation on which they can build.

I know a Catholic priest who spent time in a Zen Buddhist monastery in Japan and a Jewish rabbi who lived for a while in an ashram in India. They were able to gain new insights into their Catholicism and Judaism by viewing them through the eyes of another tradition. Being grounded in their own traditions, they had a foundation on which to build their new practices and an ongoing spiritual life in which to integrate their new insights. They did not lose their way as Bill did.

That, at least, has been my experience, too. I have already described how I trained in a classical form of Japanese martial arts, rooted in Zen Buddhism, with a traditional Japanese sensei. I also became acquainted with various Tibetan monasteries and retreat houses in the Northeast. I found myself powerfully attracted to the Tibetan tradition and I spent a couple of years immersing myself in Tibetan texts and practices.

Some found this attraction inexplicable. I remember sitting with another speaker at a conference on Buddhism and psychotherapy being held at a Tibetan monastery in Woodstock, New York. It was replete with an immense golden statue of the Buddha, colorful tapestries covering every wall, and candles burning everywhere. This psychologist, one of the leading spokespersons for Buddhist practice within psychotherapy, leaned over and said to me something like, "I can't stand this place, it reminds me too much of Saint Patrick's Cathedral where I was an alter boy." I, on the other hand, was lured by this devotionally intense and philosophically rigorous form of liturgical Buddhism. I was a high church Anglican and this was high church Buddhism.

But I wanted to remain within the Christian tradition. And a suspicion of authority and anti-institutionalism that had dogged my earlier conversion to Christianity re-appeared. I did not want to completely apprentice myself to a specific teacher and I could only go so far without learning the Tibetan language. But my time spent looking into the world of Tibetan Buddhism sparked a dialogue within myself (and sometimes with colleagues) between Buddhism and Christianity. A dialogue that is still going on between my "Buddhist self" and my "Christian self," out of which has come this book and the many ways described here in which my Christian practice has been enriched by Buddhist practices and ways of thinking.

Other Christian Spiritual Practices

Besides the ancient practice of reciting the Jesus Prayer in time with your breathing, another form of Christian meditation is the "Centering Prayer" developed by Thomas Keating. Here too the practitioner repeats a single word or phrase, again often in tune with her heartbeat. But the importance of the phrase lies not in its meaning (or its pure sound), but in the intention it expresses toward God. For Keating the center of the person is the will and so meditative prayer should center the individual on God through an act of intention. Keating recommends quietly repeating words such as "love" or "peace." Besides centering the individual on God, such a practice also strengthens our capacity for "watchfulness" or "mindfulness"—the capacity for detached observation. This enables us to maintain a more consistent focus on spiritual realities and a more constant intention to act in a loving, compassionate, and truthful way.

But it does not happen overnight. In this era of instant messaging, high-speed cable, and quick-acting drugs, we have been conditioned to want immediate results in everything we do. Contemplative disciplines such as mindfulness meditation and Centering Prayer promise no overnight delivery. Just the reverse. The fruits of contemplative disciplines will take months, even years to show up. However, over the years Keating's simple practice has been taught to thousands, and its practitioners report a deepening of their spiritual life, a more profound sense of the presence of God, and an increased ethical seriousness.

Another ancient form of Christian practice that is finding renewed interest is the traditional monastic discipline of *Lectio Divina* ("Sacred Reading"). Here you begin from the text of the Scripture and read it in a special way. Actually the focus is not on reading but on listening. Or on reading the text so that you can listen to it in a deeper way. This is a practice of *contemplative* reading and, like all contemplative practices, it develops our capacity for attention.

In *Lectio,* the text is not read for intellectual understanding or doctrinal instruction. The question is not, Can I believe what the text says? The question is, rather, What might the text be saying to me here and now? First you get into a relaxed, meditative state, perhaps by doing breathing meditation or listening briefly to beautiful music. In *Lectio,* you approach the text in a quiet and receptive mood. Then you read a short passage from the Scripture to yourself out loud, stopping often for it settle in. The point is not to cover a lot of textual ground. You read slowly and carefully until something strikes you personally. Then you stop and reflect, turning the phrase or passage over and over in your mind. You may find yourself stopping to reflect after only a sentence or two, and that reflection may take up your whole meditation time for that day.

The kinds of questions you might ask yourself focus on what the text seems to be saying to you now. What images does it evoke? What feelings and visceral sensations arise? What associations come to mind? Am I avoiding something in my dialogue with this text? As in all contemplative practices, the purpose of *Lectio* is growth in our capacity for silence, for attention, for listening. The goal, as always, is personal transformation and deeper wisdom and insight.

This is a radically different approach to reading than is common in our culture. In this era of speed-reading courses, books are treated as a commodity to be consumed as quickly as possible (and then often discarded). Quantity often takes precedence over quality. Books are seen as repositories of bits of data to be extracted as quickly and efficiently as possible so that we can accumulate more bits of data than our competitors. Or we read for titillation and entertainment. The novel becomes another means of escape, of anaesthetizing ourselves from the pressures of modern life and their impact upon us. Savoring a text, letting it address us instead of subjecting it to our will, does not come naturally to us. Since it is neither information-gathering nor entertainment, at first contemplative reading often feels strange and, like any new practice, takes time to become comfortable.

Also in our culture, the Bible is the most contested of books. Scholarly debates about its origin and interpretation have left the university classroom and become the subject of best-selling books, celebratory talk shows, and popular magazine articles. Partisans with various and conflicting opinions snatch phrases and vignettes out of context to support their own ideologies, raising a cacophony of warring interpretations. To put aside our preconceptions about the Bible, to listen for a voice lurking beneath the superficial and the obvious, will require some time and practice with the personal discipline of contemplative reading.

But no special skill is required. Any of us can learn to settle our minds, read slowly, and reflect on what we read. When persisted in with discipline, its practitioners report that *Lectio Divina* produces new insights, profound personal reorientation, and a deeper awareness of the divine presence.

Another disciplined way of approaching the scriptural text is through the use of imagery. Take a particularly poignant story and, in your mind's eye, place yourself there. Imagine you are one of the children Jesus takes in his arms, or that you are Peter when he realizes that he has denied his Master, or that you are one of the disciples at the Last Supper. What does that feel like? How do you respond to what you see and hear with your inner eyes and ears? What would you say to Jesus or Peter? What occurs to you that they would say back? How are you different after sitting at the feet of Jesus or witnessing the Crucifixion from a distance? Such active use of imagery also has a long history. For example, in the Middle Ages, Ignatious of Loyola, the founder of the Catholic Jesuit Order, constructed a set of "Spiritual Exercises" built around such practices. Those who regularly engage in such imagistic activities as part of their spiritual life often report very moving and personally transformative experiences.

Worship as Spiritual Practice

The importance of disciplined practice for deeper understanding is not only true of the various forms of meditation and devotional reading; it is also true, I think, of the liturgical life of the church or synagogue or temple. We can think of communal worship as a spiritual practice like mindfulness meditation, yogic postures, Tai-Chi, or personal Bible reading and prayer.

For communal worship to function as a spiritual discipline that leads to new ways of seeing requires, clearly, actual participation. The term "liturgy" comes from the Greek word that means work. Like any spiritual discipline, one cannot simply be passive and inert. Anyone who has tried Centering Prayer or mindfulness meditation or zazen knows that while the meditator looks passive and inert from the outside, inside the mind is awake and alert. This is true even at the neurophysiological level: the brain waves associated with a meditative state reflect concentration, not sleep, stupor, or coma. There is a paradox here: a passivity that is really activity.

Likewise the discipline of liturgical participation requires attention, concentration, and focus. As distinct from sitting and meditating, here there is activity—singing, reading, speaking, sometimes dancing or processing. But it is a paradoxical kind of activity: an activity that is really a passivity, a receptivity—allowing music, chant, symbols of flame and image and word to wash over you; allowing them to be breathed like a mantra, to be absorbed into the body and the spirit like bread that is eaten; allowing them to grasp us like a compelling poem or painting; allowing them to catch us up like a powerful drama. Like any spiritual practice, liturgical participation requires a kind of mindfulness, a cultivating of attention, a shift in states of consciousness toward a greater openness, receptivity.

Like any spiritual practice, liturgical participation does not bear fruit in an hour, or day, or week, or month. Discipline is necessary because we are temporal creatures, we live in time. That temporality means that learning, growth, and transformation take time. One lesson does not make us a concert violinist or a trained martial artist. One hour of sitting zazen does not make us enlightened. One hour of sitting in church does not make us new creatures in Christ. Liturgical participation is another example of a spiritual practice and, like any spiritual discipline, it requires consistency, attentiveness, and active participation in order to bear fruit.

In summary, this chapter has argued that knowing requires doing: that the concepts of Christian belief make little sense apart from the context of Christian practice, and that Christian faith should begin from Christian spiritual discipline rather than intellectual assent to creedal affirmations. Various spiritual disciplines like reciting the Jesus Prayer, Centering Prayer, *Lectio Divina,* active imagination, and liturgical participation can evoke that knowledge (in a "firsthand" sense) that we stand in relationship to the encompassing divine reality to which Jesus pointed.

CHAPTER TWO

The Paradoxical Presence

Encountering God

Christian spiritual practices aim at facilitating and deepening our encounter with God. Having suggested that today Christianity should begin with such practices, the next step is describing what that encounter with God might be like. In this chapter there is only one aspect of that encounter that I want to focus on—the tension between presence and absence in the experience of God. For that tension goes right to the heart of the divine reality as Christians have known it.

Divine Presence

The twentieth-century Jewish philosopher Martin Buber wrote in his book *I and Thou*.

> Man [*sic*] receives, and what he receives is not a "content" but a presence, a presence as strength. . . . And this is the inexpressible confirmation of meaning. It is guaranteed. Nothing, nothing can henceforth be meaningless.

Not content but presence. At the heart of religious experience is a sense of presence. Not primarily ideas to believe or duties to perform but an awareness of a greater presence that gives meaning to our lives.

This immediately raises a possible question for spiritual discernment—Where do *you* experience a deeper, greater presence in and behind and through your everyday life?

This question, in turn, points out something very important about the current cultural context in which our spiritual practices take place. We live in a culture where the final authority on any topic—politics, morality, art, education, religion—is our own experience. This may be good or bad. Many religious leaders, from Pope John Paul II to the current Dalai Lama, have been critical of this aspect of modern culture. It can make for superficiality, a naïve refusal to learn from the wisdom of the past, and a lack of discipline and commitment, especially in the spiritual quest. Still, something is acceptable to us today to the extent that it resonates with our own experience.

This, of course, makes building a bridge between spirituality and psychotherapy easier. Psychotherapists are primarily concerned about human experience: their patient's and their own. Such therapists are often less concerned about religious doctrines, rituals, and moral codes than they are with human experience. To the extent that spiritual practices enrich, expand, and deepen human experience, they should be of interest to those who think psychologically. That recognition that spiritual practices can enrich and expand human experience is one of the reasons for the increasing interest in spirituality on the part of psychotherapists today.

A contemporary Christian spirituality must start from experience. Hence the question, Where do you *experience* a larger, deeper reality? Where do you find a greater presence? In intimate conversations with friends? In the soaring liturgies of the church, synagogue, or temple? In compelling stories and sayings from the Holy Scriptures? In the service of the cause of peace and justice? In being caught up in the symmetries and harmonies of art and music?

For me, and many patients whose stories I hear, the answer is increasingly "in nature." I am very fortunate to live beside the Atlantic Ocean and to be writing this with the sound of the surf in the background. When I need a break from writing in order to think, often I will take a walk along the beach—even in the dead of February, when ice forms along the boardwalk and the sharpness of the wind necessitates a winter parka. Increasingly these walks have taken on a contemplative air so that, along with the liturgical life of the Church and times of solitary meditation, they have come to feel like a spiritual practice.

But what makes a practice meditative or spiritual? Not simply that it talks about God. I worked briefly in a state hospital for the chronically mentally ill. There, virtually all the patients talked about God, or to God, or claimed they were God, or Jesus, or the Virgin Mary. Talking about God is not always religious discourse. What makes discourse religious is that it discloses a sense of presence—a deeper, greater presence.

Is sitting in church (something I do virtually every week) or synagogue or temple a religious experience? Does it evoke a sense of greater presence? That is what all of the rituals is designed to do. The singing, clapping, reading, burning incense, chanting, being surrounded by stained glass, sculptures, paintings—all are designed to evoke a certain kind of experience.

They are designed to make us aware that we live in more than one world. We live in the physical world of the five senses, of space and time and tables and chairs. And we also exist in relationship to the experience of a larger, deeper, divine reality whether we are conscious of it or not. This awareness of our living relationship to a greater, more encompassing presence makes a connection between traditional spiritualities and the current psychological concern of finding meaning and purpose in our lives. This sense that our individual lives are being lived in a larger, sacred context that extends beyond our separate egos is precisely what gives our lives meaning and purpose. As Buber says, such a sense of presence is "the inexpressible confirmation of meaning . . . nothing can henceforth be meaningless."

This raises another question for spiritual discernment. We might take some time to consider how such an experience of divine presence might impact on our view of ourselves and our lives as citizens, parents, workers, devotees of a religious tradition. Certainly this experience of the presence of a larger, deeper, sacred reality impacts my work as a psychologist, my understanding of my role as a teacher, and how I think about social and political issues. For me, the psychic arm-wrestling, the moments of hopelessness, the times of breakthrough, the long periods of stagnation and groping, and all the other vicissitudes of psychotherapy participate in a larger context of sacred presence in which death can lead to rebirth—a theme we will return to in a later chapter.

Often I am asked about how I can spend so much of my work life in close proximity to men who have lost their jobs, women who have been beaten by their partners, young adults abused as children. There are many answers to this question. One is found in my knowledge that passing through death can lead to rebirth; that the path out of a situation of suffering often leads through the suffering and beyond it. This trajectory of hope is at the heart of the Christian Gospel.

Or, the struggle for justice in society is part of the ongoing plan of God to transform the kingdoms of this world into a closer approximation of the Kingdom of God. Those who work for justice know that their actions are in line with the ultimate course of history, however distant that Kingdom of God appears. Part of the function of the spiritual life is to place our strivings for justice, our desire for wisdom, our longing for love and compassion in an encompassing and meaning-giving embrace.

This is one thing on which all the religions of the world agree—that we live in at least two worlds. The two worlds are called by many different names: time and eternity, matter and spirit, finite and infinite, samsara (the world of suffering) and nirvana (the world of peace), maya (illusion) and Brahma (the true nature of things).

These two worlds of which the religious traditions speak do not always feel congruent to me. In a previous book I quoted the following account of one contemporary description of the experience of these two worlds:

> Another experience happened to me . . . the evening of the day before my son was born. My first child had been still-born and, as I lay in bed, I was very anxious about my wife and much disturbed in mind. And then a great peace came over me. I was conscious of a lovely, unexplainable pattern in the whole texture of things, a pattern of which everyone and everything was a part; and weaving the pattern was a Power; and that Power was what we faintly call Love. I realized that we are not lonely atoms in a cold, unfriendly, indifferent universe, but that each of us is linked up in a rhythm, of which we may be unconscious, and which we can never really know but to which we can submit ourselves trustfully and unreservedly.

And so he concludes that he knows that everything will be all right.

This seems to me a fundamentally religious sense: that I am related to a greater reality, a larger pattern of which I am a part. This results in knowing that everything will be all right. It may very well not be all right in this sensory world of tables and chairs, but there is a larger reality in which we can trust, of which we are a part. In that more encompassing reality in which the vicissitudes of life are taken up, everything will be all right.

Yet in my everyday life things are so far from being all right. Sickness, poverty, crime, greed, violence confront me on every side. And I must confess that I do not know how to keep these two truths, these two worlds, in balance. None of the pious cliches that people offer really satisfy my mind or heart. There are many clouds in which I can discern no silver lining, and many doors that people said were opened by God that led them to a dead end.

I suspect that there is no intellectually satisfying answer to the question of how to hold together these two experiences—a transcendental sense of harmony and tranquility and a quotidian world of violence and suffering. Perhaps the only way to find the answer is through the *practice* of living in both worlds.

This sense of living in at least two worlds is central to the spiritual life. The nineteenth-century Danish philosopher Søren Kierkegaard once said that the riddle of life is how to live in eternity when you still hear the clock strike. Clocks don't strike any more, but the point remains. It is hard to maintain any focus or give any attention to the "eternal" when we live so much in the world of deadlines, clocks ticking away, schedules confining us, responsibilities calling to us. Maybe there was once a time in the ancient, distant past when time and eternity, the particularities of life and the more encompassing presence, were present together. But we do not live in such a time now. For us the train schedule, the newscast, the kids' activities press upon us. To also live in relationship to eternity calls on us to live with a peculiarly divided consciousness.

And we cannot underestimate the psychological difficulty of living with such a split awareness today. Sometimes I feel quite crazy holding onto my convictions about the reality of the spiritual dimension of experience when I walk through the halls of the university where virtually every colleague I meet from physics, biology, psychology, and philosophy insists that the only reality is the material world. I feel equally peculiar affirming a greater, divine reality when a younger colleague is struck with cancer, or one of my students is randomly and brutally raped, or I read about whole villages of children dying of starvation in the third world. There is very little in my everyday experience that supports the spiritual convictions by which I try to lead my life.

But this is what separates the religious from the non-religious person today. Not so much a set of beliefs or even practices (people meditate, for example, just to lower their blood pressure; or go to church just for social support). What separates the religious from the nonreligious person today is the experience that there is more to reality than just matter and time, physics and chemistry.

Many may disagree with me at this point. But I am not one of those people who think that everything is necessary spiritual. Everything we do may, in some sense, be potentially spiritual, but that is not always necessarily so. In my vocabulary just because something makes me feel good, actualizes my true self, or reaches out to another, does not necessarily make it spiritual. Thoughts and actions can be good, wonderful, necessary and still not be automatically spiritual.

There is a tendency today to stretch the term "spiritual" in so many directions that it becomes impossible to know what it means. Confucius talked about the "rectification of names" and I want to keep the name "spiritual" for what I think is a necessary dimension of human life—the experience of standing in relationship to a greater, sacred presence. At its most minimal, I think, any spirituality (and especially a Christian one) must affirm that we, and the world around us, are not simply a random assortment of atoms and molecules but that there is a greater, sacred, infinitely mysterious reality present in us and to us.

Again, this is one of the things on which all the religions of the world agree—that we are not just creatures of space and time, biology, and chemistry. Rather there is within each of us and within our friends and lovers, our children, and our worst adversaries, a soul or spirit or Atman or Buddha nature.

Every religion has some variant of the opening of the Book of Genesis that says that we are made in the image of God. In Hinduism, for example, through the disciplines of yoga and meditation, we are able to pierce through the veil of ignorance and see that we are one with the divine reality. In Christianity we can see our divine image reflected in the divine image made flesh in Jesus—Irenaeus, a theologian of the earliest Christian centuries, wrote, "He became like us that we might become like him."

As Søren Kierkegaard said, "we are finite beings with an infinite desire" or, perhaps, a desire for the infinite. Hundreds of years before, Saint Augustine said something similar when he said that our hearts are restless until they rest in God. Augustine and Kierkegaard are talking about desire. Spirituality comes to us not primarily as concepts or duties, but as desire. Our natural desire is to enter into a conscious relationship with the source of our life. The task of spiritual practice is to enable this desire to follow its natural course and reach its most fulfilling end.

Often the two worlds of which the religions speak are thought of as antagonists: a conflict of flesh and spirit, maya and Brahma. But that is not necessary. They may also be thought of as two directions of desire: toward the frantic world of checkbooks, automobiles, and advertising images on the TV; and toward the still world that surrounds the everyday and in which our lives find a home. That desire of which Augustine and Kierkegaard speak finds its rest in the experience of divine presence. This longing for God is not opposed to our normal experience but rather arises from within the world of our desire. These two trajectories of desire are not necessarily opposed, as long as one does not crowd out the other. And living life fully may require attention to both.

Some psychologists (Freud, for example) argue that such a desire for God is only the child's desire for its parents writ large. Such a claim gains credence from the fact that this divine presence is often described with images from the parent-child relationship. In many religions the divine reality is described as "Father" or "Mother." On one hand, if a person's religious experience is going to make sense to them and be integrated into their life, it must be internally connected to the basic themes of their personal history. One such theme in many peoples' lives is the wish for an all-loving or perfect and ideal parent. The psychoanalysis of religion does lay bare the wishes, fears, and other psychological dynamics carried by all our religious convictions, our atheistic assertions, and our philosophies of life. To that extent, Freud is right: religion does express the wishes and dynamics of the psyche, often including those derived from our childhood experiences with our parents and including the wish to merge with an all-loving mother or please and be protected by an all-powerful father.

On the other hand, the truthfulness of claims about the divine existence and reality cannot be settled by appeals to their psychological origin, as Freud himself recognized. Freud's militant atheism was compelling to him in part because it fit with his own personal history and psychological dynamics and at that level was no different from the piety he so opposed. Freud was the first in a long line of psychologists who were rightly eager to subject religion to the most intense psychological scrutiny but then refused to subject their militant atheism to the same analysis. Just as there are neurotic reasons for believing in God—and there certainly are many—so also there are neurotic reasons for refusing to believe in God. One may reject God out of rebellion against his parents. Another may stay clear of any religion because she wishes her will alone to rule her life. The question of whether or not there are good reasons to embrace a spiritual path or reject it cannot be settled by psychology alone.

Also, the fact that a wish or desire may have its roots in childhood does not necessarily mean that it is infantile. A child's curiosity and continual interrogation of her parents about "why is the sky blue" and "why does the dog bark" may drive her parents crazy. Later in life it may develop into the motivation to spend hours in the laboratory and to make a Nobel Prize–winning discovery. A child banging on a toy piano may disrupt the household. Later in life it may develop into the discipline needed to be a concert performer and composer.

I may need the love of another at the age of four and again at fourteen and yet again at fifty-four. But the nature of that need and that love is no longer the child's need for a parent or the infatuation of adolescence, although it is in continuity with them. No one says that hard-won scientific discoveries or virtuoso concert performances or mature intimacies are infantile because they have roots in childhood. Likewise, adult spiritual practice may grow out of desires begun in childhood, but that does not make it childish.

The Negative Way

So far we have talked about spirituality, especially from a Christian perspective, as involving presence—the presence in us and to us of a sacred and meaning-giving reality. To speak only of presence, however, is too simple, too "once born," in William James' words. The spiritual life is not only made up of times of ecstatic presence, of "once I was blind but now I see." If I have a criticism of much so-called New Age spirituality it is here. Such spirituality is often too "once born," with too little sense of the darker side of the spiritual journey—the dark nights of the soul, the wanderings in the wilderness, the desert times, the cries of "My God, my God, why have you forsaken me?" Any spirituality of the presence of God must be balanced by a spirituality of the absence of the presence of God or the presence of the absence of God. Carl Jung once said that we become enlightened not by meditating on the light (which seems to be the New Age way), but by facing up to "the shadow," the darkness, the loss.

Times of enlightenment, of "once I was blind and now I see," are often followed by times that the fourteenth-century Christian text appropriately called *The Cloud of Unknowing* describes as follows,

> It is usual to find nothing but a darkness around your mind, or, as it were, a cloud of unknowing. You will know nothing and feel nothing except a simple reaching out to God in the depths of your being. No matter what you do, this darkness and this cloud will remain between you and your God. You will feel frustrated, for your mind will be unable to grasp him. Learn to be at home in this darkness. Return to it as often as you can. . . . If in this life you hope to feel and see God at all, it must be within this darkness and this cloud (chapter III).

Classically, Christians have called this the *via negativa,* the way of negation; Buddhists call it the way of emptiness.

This approach to spirituality flows naturally from the nature of the divine reality. The Chinese classic, the *Tao te Ching* opens with the magnificent words, "The Tao that can be named is not the real Tao." In Christian terms, we might say that the God that can be named is not the real God. The God that can be named is an idol, a projection, a creation of the human mind put in the place of God. Thus the prohibition that anchors the Law of Moses: "you shall not make any images." Not just images of stone or wood but also images of word and concept. The true God is beyond all images, no matter how pious or how abstract. The early-twentieth-century theologian Karl Barth insists that God reveals God's self but remains hidden at the same time, that the revelation of God does not negate the hiddenness of God. Religious concepts and forms, however pious and spiritual sounding, easily turn to idols. How often religious folk seem to make idols of a creed, a book, a liturgy, an ethical code, a tradition and worship it instead of the God to whom they point.

This experience of the *via negativa,* entering that "Cloud of Unknowing," may appear to rob us of the religious ideas and symbols we hold dear.

> But now you put to me a question and say, How might I think of him in himself, and what is he? And to this I can only answer thus, I have no idea. For with your question you have brought me into the same darkness, into that same cloud of unknowing where I wish you were myself. . . . No man can think of God himself. Therefore it is my choice to leave behind everything that I can think of and choose for my love that which I cannot think. For why: He may well be loved but not thought. He can be taken and held by love but not by thought (chapter VI).

Longing and love reach where reasoning, analyzing, and moralizing cannot go. Thinking can only take us so far. Then desire and love must take over. "With a devout and a pleasing stirring of love, strive to pierce that darkness above you. You are to smite upon that thick cloud of unknowing with a sharp dart of longing love" (chapter VI). God attracts, God does not coerce. Our natural longing for a loving union with our Source lures us forward. The spiritual life comes to us not primarily as duty or argument but as desire and love. Human desire is not the enemy of the spiritual life but just the reverse. Desire is the wellspring and motivation for taking up a spiritual practice. Through the disciplines of the spiritual journey, our deepest desires are not repressed or denied but are rather facilitated and allowed to expand infinitely.

However, as part of the process of entering the cloud of unknowing, all other ideas and practices, no matter how devout, must be put aside.

> If ever you come to this cloud, and live and work in it as I bid you, just as this cloud of unknowing is above you, between you and your God, in the same way you must put beneath you a cloud of forgetting, between you and all the creatures that have ever been made. . . . I make no exceptions, whether they are bodily creatures or spiritual . . . whether these be good or evil (chapter V).

This applies not just to those objects unrelated to religion but even those considered most spiritual.

> Therefore, though it is at times good to think of the kindness and worthiness of God in particular. And though this is a light and a part of contemplation, nevertheless, in this exercise, it must be cast down and covered over with a cloud of forgetting. You are to step above it stalwartly but lovingly (chapter VI).

No matter how truthful or pious a thought or image or object is, it is to be lovingly but firmly put under foot as a distraction from the experience of that divine reality that is beyond all words and images and forms.

This is not to suggest that the ordinary practices of the Christian life or our natural affections for people and objects in our ordinary world should be completely suppressed or forgotten. "I want you to reckon each thought and each impulse," he writes, "at its proper value" (chapter XI). The author continually stresses the importance of religious discipline and writes that it is often appropriate to reflect upon one's life and the world around one. "But in this exercise it profits little or nothing" (chapter V). In order "to feel and see God as he is in himself" it is necessary to enter "this darkness and this cloud" in which everything else fades into the background.

Such a process is far from easy or painless. The contemporary Thomas Merton writes, "If we set out into this darkness, we have to meet these inexorable forces. We will have to face fears and doubts. We will have to call into question the whole structure of our spiritual lives" (Merton, 1973: 96). Later he calls this a process "that risks intolerable purifications, and sometimes, indeed very often, the risk turns out to be too great to be tolerated" (1966: 58). Such states of consciousness are difficult, almost unbearable, for "We do not find it easy to subsist in a void in which our natural powers have nothing of their own to rely on"

(1961: 135). This negative way leads to loss, and loss can lead to grief and mourning.

Freud understood in his book *Mourning and Melancholia* that mourning and anger are connected. However irrational it may seem, we may feel enraged at the parent, lover, friend, or relative whom we mourn. So likewise, in the dark night of the soul, in the midst of the cloud of unknowing, we may rage at the hidden God who seems to have forsaken us.

In a coming chapter we are going to speak about how loss and mourning are essential aspects of the spiritual quest, that loss and mourning are necessary for rebirth and growth. Entering into the cloud of unknowing, embracing the hiddeness of God, involves this loss and mourning of familiar religious forms. Presumably that is why we may recoil from it. We do not want to grieve and mourn for the religious enlightenments we have known. Earlier in our spiritual journey we may have felt that we understood about God. Now we realize we did not and cannot. "You will feel frustrated," the author of *The Cloud of Unknowing* assures us, "for your mind will be unable to grasp" the divine reality.

The *via negativa* begins from and returns to the ordinary routines of the Christian (or some other) tradition: its creeds, texts, rituals, and symbols. Gradually, after a time of living and working with them, these forms may begin to lose their former profundity. Part of the power of a spiritual practice is that when done consistently, it pushes us to the limits of that very practice itself. Liturgical worship may become too familiar and grow stale. Sitting and meditating may eventually become dull. Intellectual activity may lose its attraction after many years in the library. Rather than signaling a loss of faith, such dark moments may indicate that the Christian seeker is coming to the limits of any finite formula in the face of the ultimate. Every liturgy, every word, every symbol, every practice is finite and limited and eventually loses its meaning in the face of the infinity of God. Thus the *via negativa* arises out of traditional Christian practices taken to their limit.

That is why the negative way is not a kind of cheap mysticism that avoids the disciplines of rigorous thought and spiritual practice in order to take refuge in the slogan that the experience of God is beyond words. Yes, the divine reality is beyond words. But we only *know* as a part of our lived experience that that is true by engaging in a disciplined practice and letting it take us slowly and painfully to, and beyond, its limits.

Psychologically the *via negativa* involves the willingness to go beyond familiar religious forms—often driven beyond them by the trajectory of the experiences these practices have created—into the void. But these religious forms are not simply outgrown or left behind as though this was a normal process of growing up or the result of skepticism about religious faith. The author of *The Cloud of Unknowing* insists that his reader continue in the regular practices of the Christian Church even while moving beyond them (chapter XXXV).

Instead, the regular forms of Christian faith—the creeds, texts, symbols, and rituals—cease to be valued as ends in themselves. They are now embraced only as means to a greater end, to what the desert fathers in Christianity called "pure prayer" or "imageless prayer," in other words, to that cloud of unknowing wherein God is known as God by not being known (in a conventional sense) at all.

Entering the cloud of unknowing, the Christian seeker goes beyond all religious forms—casting them down and covering them over with a cloud of forgetting, stepping above them stalwartly but lovingly (chapter VI). While no longer identified with the divine reality, which is beyond all possible identifications, prayers and texts and symbols are still valued as part of the larger context of practice in which the spiritual seeker lives. In the classical texts like *The Cloud,* the traditional objects of belief are not lost, rejected, or given up, but rather given a new context. The creeds, symbols, and sacred texts are taken seriously but not absolutely.

No doubt this is a very difficult stance to maintain: to value the forms of religion without making them into absolutes. Those who confuse fanaticism with devotion refuse to do this, preferring instead to demand submission to what they see as absolute. Likewise, those who reject all religious beliefs and practices refuse to look beyond them to their more encompassing Source. But among those who can maintain this difficult stance, religious texts and teachings are no longer seen as divine themselves; but religious texts and teachings and disciplines are still cherished as parts of the Christian's life of practice.

Arising out of the disciplines of the Christian life, the cloud of unknowing itself constitutes a further discipline. "Learn to be at home in this darkness. Return to it as often as you can"—this speaks of a practice, not an episodic event. And there is no surpassing it, no stage beyond it.

> There never yet existed, nor ever shall be, so pure a creature, one so ravished on high in contemplation and love of the godhead, who did not find this high and wonderful cloud of unknowing between him and his God (chapter XVII).

Even the most experienced adept remains under the cloud of unknowing.

When Loss is Gain

Is it all loss, this experience of the hiddenness of God? Is there no gain? Yes, of course there is gain. There are at least three areas of gain that can come from the negative way.

First, there is gain in terms of our facing reality. In the *via negativa* we are coming face to face with the reality of God. Not an idol at our beck and call, not the infantile fulfiller of our most cherished wishes that Freud ridiculed in his book *The Future of An Illusion,* but the reality of the Absolute, which we can only experience as emptiness; the Absolute, which remains hidden even while being revealed; the reality that "My ways are not your ways, says the Lord"; the reality "that it is a terrifying thing to fall into the hands of the living God." The *via negativa* is not for cowards.

The second gain that can come from the *via negativa* today concerns the fact that people raised in religious traditions have often learned to associate certain images of God with very unpleasant experiences. Following are two examples.

The other day I was going through the supermarket. There was a young boy running wildly down the isle. He turned the corner, ran up the next isle and from behind the shelves I heard the inevitable sound of canned goods crashing to the floor. Immediately I heard his mother's voice shout, "God will punish you if you do that again!" "There's another atheist in the making," I said to myself. Sometimes in my classes I ask students to simply relate their associations to the words "religion" or "God." The majority reflect the image I call "God, the cosmic scorekeeper," a divine parent always looking out for any infraction.

Often people raised in the Christian Church grow up with a very punitive image of God. To speak of God evokes aversive experiences of judgment, guilt, and condemnation. They cannot think about God without experiencing these feelings. This is what I call "affectively induced atheism." Rather than suffer these affects of pain and guilt, people simply avoid the subject of God. I suspect that more atheism results from these emotional causes than from all the philosophical objections to belief in God.

One way out of this affectively induced atheism is the imageless experience of God, which, because it is imageless, does not evoke those painful and destructive feelings of self-condemnation.

Another example of images of God that can create problems for us today involves masculine, patriarchal images of God. The opening books of the Hebrew Scriptures draw most of their images and symbols for God from the political-legal realm, imaging God as King, Warrior, Judge. In that culture, this political-legal-military domain was primarily the province of men. Recently, many women, and men, too, turned away from Western Religions because of these hypermasculine images of God, and are now trying to find a way to remain loyal to these traditions without being continually enraged by such patriarchal language. An experiencing of the divine beyond any images means a passing beyond all images and concepts, including concepts of gender.

Thus a second advantage of the *via negativa* today is that it allows us to encounter the divine reality without the pejorative associations that may have built up over a lifetime of religious instruction.

The third gain is that the spirituality of the *via negativa* is particularly relevant to us today. I think this is true for two reasons.

The first reason for the special relevance of the *via negativa* to our situation today comes from the parallel between the process of taking up the *via negativa* by entering the cloud of unknowing and the history of religion in modern Western culture. In the premodern period, during the Middle Ages and the Reformation, Christianity in the West involved the affirmation of certain concrete and dogmatic beliefs about God, Christ, human nature, and the Church. In the Enlightenment period and the Age of Reason, many rejected these creedal beliefs in the name of science and rationality. For many that was, and remains, the end of the matter—the rejection of these dogmatic beliefs about God means the rejection of Christianity and of God.

In the *via negativa* the beliefs and symbols of Christianity and every religion are re-evaluated and are no longer idealized or made into absolutes. But they are not re-evaluated in the way that was done by Enlightenment skeptics and rationalists who debunked, rejected, or claimed to outgrow their religious convictions. Rather in the *via negativa* religious symbols are re-evaluated in the sense that the absolute status of all religious forms is relativized, their limitations in the face of the inexpressibility of God are revealed. Creeds and beliefs and institutions are no longer seen as themselves divine. Only God has that honor. Thus the *via negativa* represents a form of religious re-evaluation very different from that carried by the Enlightenment, with its faith in the vanquishing of religion by science.

Enlightenment critics of religion, and their modern counterparts, assume that only a few possibilities remained for religious faith in the modern world: a skeptical disenchantment with religion, which was soon to be replaced by science; a defensive holding onto a naïve and superstitious faith; or, perhaps, an abstract and overly intellectualized substitute for religion fashioned by religious intellectuals. All three responses to the Enlightenment attack on religion are well represented in contemporary society. There are many best-selling authors who debunk religion as unscientific and outdated. There are religious militants who insist on a rigid and authoritarian approach to their tradition as the only true faith. And there are philosophers of religion who speak of God in abstract terms as a cosmic energy or another name for the laws of nature.

By contrast, *The Cloud of Unknowing* and other texts within the Christian tradition of the *via negativa* speak of an experience of God "beyond affirmation and negation." Such an experience drives a wedge between the critical rejection of specific, concrete images of God and the rejection of all experience of God. The re-evaluation of specific symbols of God need not lead to a rejection of the reality of God. The *via negativa* opens up the possibility of an experience of God coexisting with the re-evaluation of all concepts and symbols about God. Thus the *via negativa* takes up where modern atheism leaves off with its rejection of specific, concrete beliefs about God.

Here a critical re-evaluation of Christian belief may lead to a deeper experience of the reality of God rather than to atheism. *The Cloud of Unknowing*, and writers like Merton, suggest that entering the void can lead the individual to a renewed and transformed Christian sensibility and practice. The *via negativa* offers a transforming religious experience that is an alternative to the skeptical rejection of religion, or naïve superstition, or an intellectualized religion of lifeless abstractions. It cannot be equated with any of them.

The second way in which the *via negativa* is especially relevant to our situation today concerns the way in which we think about the kind of language that is appropriate for discussions of religious matters. The eighteenth-century philosopher Emmanuel Kant set the stage for our current understanding of language in a book aptly entitled *Religion Within the Limits of Reason Alone*. The title says it all. Religion can only survive by confining itself within the limits of the rational. These limits included the limits of language.

Kant argues that our language is limited, caught in a prison of finitude. Human language works well to describe objects in the table-and-chair world of time and space. But such limited, finite language cannot reach beyond the physical world to any transcendental, divine reality. Our language is limited, our minds are limited, the categories of our cognitive processing system are limited and so there is no way our human language can speak about any possible divine reality. This is how modern philosophy and modern culture, following Kant, thinks about language.

Traditionally the *via negativa* was contrasted to what our ancestors called the *via positiva* (the positive way). This involved speaking directly about God. Our ancestors thought of language as being able to reach up to God like Jacob's ladder reaching up to heaven in the Hebrew Bible. After Kant, we in the modern world no longer think about language in that way.

Again the *via negativa* accepts our contemporary view of language as limited and finite. But the negative way goes on to say that there is an experience of God beyond the limits of language. As a matter of fact, the experience of God involves precisely experiencing both the limits of language and a passing beyond language.

In modern ways of thinking we do not have an understanding of language that allows us to speak directly, descriptively, about God. But that does not necessarily leave us with atheism. We can still experience that divine reality that is "beyond both affirmation and negation" through a passing beyond descriptive language.

Here I can imagine an objection from any skeptical reader: if the divine reality is beyond description, how can we know if our experience is authentic or not? How can we evaluate the truth or falsity of religious statements? The answer that religious traditions have always given to this question, as the psychologist William James noted almost a hundred years ago, is that such experiences are evaluated by their fruits. The criteria for the authenticity of religious experience are not the kind of criteria used in evaluating the results of a laboratory experiment. The criteria for the truthfulness of Christian experience is not the criteria of a philosophical naturalism that claims that the world as described by empirical science is the one and only reality. Such naturalistic criteria are designed precisely to exclude the kinds of truth claims made by Christianity or any other religion. Rather, the criteria for the authenticity of Christian experience are the moral and spiritual criteria of ongoing personal transformation. Does the experience of returning again and again to the cloud of unknowing facilitate a person's journey toward "doing justice, loving mercy, and walking humbly with God?"—that is the appropriate criteria.

So the *via negativa* has a particular relevance for us today. It liberates the experience of God from various aversive images of God that many people carry around with them. It moves our encounter with the divine reality beyond the sterile debate between those who affirm and those who deny the truth of various concepts of God. It allows for an awareness of God that is not dependent on the limitations of language.

The Heart of God

This discussion of spirituality as both presence and absence brings us close to the heart of the divine mystery: How can presence and absence coexist? My thinking about this question has been heavily influenced by my exposure to Tibetan Buddhism. For several years I have taught courses in world religions and often studied Buddhism in that context. In addition I attended retreats at a Buddhist monastery and read extensively in Buddhist texts. I also have colleagues in both religious studies and psychology who are practicing Buddhists. Late into many nights and over many cups of coffee and glasses of wine we discussed and debated the purposes of Zen sitting meditation, the nature of selfhood in Buddhism, Judaism, and Christianity, the tensions among the Theravada (the traditional Buddhism of Southeast Asia), the Mahayana (the Buddhism found in East Asian countries), and the Tibetan forms of Buddhism. Time spent in the Buddhist world and in a dialogue between Buddhism and Christianity both within myself and with colleagues led to the following reflections on the nature of the Void.

As we will discuss further in the next chapter, Buddhists say that the ultimate truth about the world is emptiness. And that emptiness expresses itself as wisdom and compassion. Emptiness, the Absence, the Void, is not an annihilating nothingness. As we will see in the next chapter, Buddhism rejects the idea of emptiness as a literal concept, an annihilation of all that is. One of my favorite Buddhist texts, the *Heart Sutra,* repeats the refrain "form is emptiness, emptiness is form." Emptiness is not empty. Rather the Void is the source of all that is. From out of the Void come wisdom and compassion and the entire cosmos.

This is strikingly parallel to the Christian doctrine of the Trinity as it was discussed in the early centuries of the Church. Many of the theologians of the Church's first centuries described the Trinity as a divine abyss (the "Father") expressing itself as compassion (the "Son") and as wisdom (the "Holy Spirit"). In theological school, I was drawn to the writings of the philosophers and theologians of the first few centuries. I found there a vision of Christianity both more experientially grounded and more philosophically rigorous than any I saw around me. I had lived with Southern Pentecostals and so had a firsthand knowledge of experiential religion. But they had no use for philosophy or psychology. And in the Boston area I met philosophical theologians possessed of immense philosophical rigor but whose writings seemed far removed from the devotional life. In the writings of the early Christian theologians I found significant philosophical analysis in combination with intense spiritual practice—the same thing I encountered again in Tibetan Buddhism.

A revered Buddhist teacher said that a misunderstanding of emptiness is like a poorly held snake or a badly cast spell. That is, it is apt to rebound and do mischief to the speaker. In Tibetan Buddhism, at a certain point in one's training, one takes Bodhisattva vows (rather like confirmation vows in some churches). One of which is a vow not to speak about emptiness to the spiritually immature. In Buddhism, then, speaking about emptiness is surrounded by warnings and taboos.

In part that is because, I think, emptiness and speech about emptiness are not about speculating over or discussing a concept called "emptiness." Rather emptiness and any speech about emptiness are a contemplative strategy. This is true of Buddhism as a whole. Buddhism is not about speculation and discourse (I get angry when I see courses offered or books written about "Buddhist Philosophy" as though it were a set of concepts). Rather Buddhism is about liberation from suffering and the transformation of awareness through spiritual discipline. Speech about emptiness is another form of spiritual practice, designed to liberate us from attachment to the world of suffering, not to fuel intellectual debates.

Likewise with the Christian doctrine of the Trinity. I often wish that it too was surrounded by warnings and taboos and that every Christian took a vow not to discuss it with the spiritually immature. For the doctrine of the Trinity too is not about intellectual debate. The doctrine of the Trinity is also a contemplative strategy, the contemplation of which can take us deep into the heart of the divine mystery. The contemplation of this mystery strikes us dumb with amazement before the reality that from an unnamable Source comes forth compassion and wisdom—the Son and the Holy Spirit—and everything we see around us.

To *speak* of such a mystery creates only words and concepts—reifications that easily become idols that separate us from each other and from our Source. The God beyond affirmation and negation is a mystery that cannot be comprehended. The amazement at an Abyss from which comes forth the cosmos we see and the compassion and wisdom that can redeem it, such amazement connects us to the mystery at the heart of reality. Such amazement strikes us dumb and renders us silent with contemplation.

Like Christianity, Buddhism also personifies these expressions of the abyss—not as a "Son" and a "Holy Spirit" but as Buddhas and Bodhisattvas and other figures of wisdom and compassion. In Southeast Asian villages can be found anthropomorphic and deified icons and statues of the Enlightened One. Japan, Korea, and Tibet are populated with additional portraits of semi-divine Buddhas and Bodhisattvas. Personalizing and anthropomorphizing are in no way limited to Christianity or absent from Buddhism. Buddhism and Christianity both contain practices of devotion to personal religious figures. Neither Buddhism or Christianity can exist on pure negation (nor can any living religion). Both Christianity and Buddhism must personify the ultimate reality.

The move into the cloud of unknowing, entering the negative way, is not a goal in itself. Rather it is part of a larger life of Christian practice that includes liturgies of worship, prayers of intercession, and works of mercy. The goal of this spiritual practice, of entering the cloud of unknowing, is not some momentary ecstasy, not simply what psychologists call a "peak experience." Rather the goal is a deeper insight into the nature of reality, a continuing awareness of the truth of everyday existence arising out of the Void. The goal of spiritual practice is not ecstatic experience but a knowing that penetrates to the heart of reality and finds there the divine source from which the physical world is generated. The world we know is not ultimate or final. The fulfillments it offers us are real and truly pleasurable but also transitory. However, that is not the last word. We are sourced and sustained by an eternal reality beyond our individual egos.

Thus, ironically, the *via negativa* is not primarily about negation. Nor is it simply a complicated way of insisting on the philosophical idea that our language cannot comprehend God. It is a practice that leads to insight into the mystery of God and the mystery of the cosmos. Not a comprehension of God or a theory about God but an insight born of practice—that emptiness and love, absence and presence, what in other places might be called the impersonal and personal aspects of God, exist together.

The *via negativa* is not only negation, it is also revelation—a disclosure of God's self-giving love in creation, in a process of compassionate transformation, in an ongoing deepening of wisdom and understanding. Again, the "Father," the "Son," and the "Holy Spirit"—a revelation by which she spreads herself throughout all of reality, becoming "all in all." The Void is also the self-manifesting creator God, and the self-manifesting creator God is also the Void. "Form is emptiness; emptiness is form." The Void is not just emptiness but is also the ever-relational source of existence. The Trinitarian God is a self-expressing, eternally relational divine reality.

Here, perhaps, Buddhism and Christianity part company. Made in the image of God, we too are relational creatures. To the extent that Buddhism insists on the ultimate extinguishing of all distinctions so that selfhood finally and completely disappears, its view of human nature is very different from the Judeo-Christian image of the self-in-relation. But stereotypes of each other's positions must be avoided. Christians can sometimes appear to be insisting on an isolated and atomistic individualism rather than a relational individualism. And Buddhists can sometimes appear to be championing an annihilating emptiness into which selfhood vanishes rather than an ultimate reality that embraces both emptiness and form. In truth Christianity and Buddhism both seek to avoid either an individualism of disconnected selves or an emptiness in which all forms simply cease. Both affirm that individual selves, like all of reality, are dependent on a more ultimate Source. And both know that these things can be experienced and known to be true through disciplined practice that is the heart of Christian and Buddhist spirituality.

CHAPTER THREE

The Cross-Legged Buddha
and the Cross-Stricken Christ

The previous chapters have drawn quite explicitly on comparisons between Christianity and Buddhism: contrasting their approaches to meditation and spiritual practice, using Buddhist concepts to gain new insights into Christian doctrines like the Trinity. This discussion is part of a larger dialogue between Christians and Buddhists that has been going on for many decades. To deepen this discussion, this chapter will explore some of the interfaces between Christianity and Buddhism. It will focus on some of the ways in which both traditions are committed to spiritual practices, ethical living, intellectual reflection, and to the development of new teachings and doctrines.

The radically secularized world of contemporary culture reduces knowledge to sound-bites, smothers disciplined reflection with celebrity and entertainment, and drives out moral and religious deliberation with technical discourse. In the public domain religions, especially Christianity and Buddhism, have been simplified and oversimplified by their noisiest and most media-savvy partisans. The two-thousand-year sweep of Christian life and practice has been boiled down to a simple "born again" sloganeering and a few moralistic Biblical clichés. Complex and colorful Buddhist traditions have been reduced to one or two private meditational techniques. When I listen to students in the classroom or hear discussions on the radio, I often suspect that contemporary American Christians and Buddhists have little acquaintance with the richness and diversity of their own traditions. Because I think this is the case, in this chapter I want to indicate some of the many different ways Christians and Buddhists, especially at the beginning of their religions, have understood themselves and the practices they engaged in.

In any discussion of Buddhism and Christianity it is important never to lose sight of the fact that both Christianity and Buddhism are internally very diverse. One can never compare "Christianity" and "Buddhism" but rather a local expression of a rich and diverse tradition with another local expression of another rich and diverse tradition. Many of the terms that are central in the current Buddhist-Christian discussion—such as no-self, God, nirvana—are understood very differently by different schools within Buddhism and Christianity. These traditions differ greatly within themselves as well as between each other. How fruitful the dialogue between them is depends in part on which groups are taken as the representatives of Christianity and of Buddhism. An unfruitful dialogue can be staged if a very narrow and fundamentalist Protestantism is compared with Southeast Asian Theravada or Japanese Zen. Or parallels are easily drawn when liberal Protestantism is compared with Pure Land Buddhism. Or, to my mind, compelling insights are generated when Mahayana and Vajrayana philosophies and practices are discussed in relation to the full range of the Christian tradition, from the earliest theologians to present thinkers.

Also any discussion between Buddhism and Christianity must not compare the popular or devotional language of one tradition with the philosophical or conceptually refined language of the other. Buddhism and Christianity each contains the experience-near and emotionally rich languages necessary for popular religious devotions and practices. Each also displays complex intellectual discourses used for conceptual clarification and philosophical discussion. Both types of language are necessary for a living religion. But interreligious dialogue must keep them straight or create inevitable misunderstandings. Sophisticated Buddhist reflections on the nature of mind must not be juxtaposed with mass-marketed Protestant devotions. New Age popularizations of supposedly Tantric Buddhist techniques, suitable for weekend workshops, must not be compared with medieval mystical teachings on the reality of God. To do so is to confuse two very different types of religious practice.

The larger context of this current Buddhist-Christian encounter is the increasing anomie, escapism, and materialism of much of contemporary Westernized cultures—trends that can be seen as easily in Japan as in North America. Such an ethos equally undermines both Christianity and Buddhism. The present discussion between them should involve ways of addressing this global ethos that powerfully impacts on the adherents of both traditions.

The Awakened and the Anointed

Accounts disagree about exactly when Prince Siddhartha who was to become known as the "Buddha" (which means "Awakened One"), was born. Indian, Chinese, and Southeast Asian sources give different dates, and even different centuries, for his birth, spanning the fourth to the second century before the common era. The early Buddhist texts tell us little about his childhood. There is general agreement that he was born to a princely family in northeastern India, that his mother died shortly after he was born, that he was raised in opulence, married as an adolescent, and soon became the father of a son.

His birth is surrounded with miraculous stories, including that astrologers told his father that Siddhartha was destined to be either a great king or a great religious leader. His father, himself a king, knew which of those destinies was best for his son and so kept the boy in a palace full of youth and beauty and music and all the other pleasures of the world. Thus protected from any unhappiness and fully satiated, the king was sure his son would develop no interest in spiritual matters.

Not until the age of twenty-one does Prince Siddhartha venture beyond his palace of delight. There, according to tradition, he sees the "four passing sights": an old man, a sick man, and a dead man on the way to burial. It is said that for the first time in his life Siddhartha encounters old age, sickness, and death and finds out that they are the inevitable destiny of human beings. He then sees the fourth sight: an ascetic who has renounced pleasure in the search to transcend the world of suffering. Shattered by the realization of what life finally holds for him, in that moment the protected prince decides to renounce the transitory pleasures of the world and become an ascetic too.

In a scene dramatized in a thousand different Buddhist stories and pictures, Prince Siddhartha leaves his young wife and infant son, refuses to obey his father's command to remain at home, turns his back on the world of pleasure and sets out to find a path that will liberate him from the world of suffering. For six years, tradition says, he engages in the austere ascetic practices common in India at this time. But such harsh mortifications bring him no relief.

One moonlit night, after meditating all night under a tree, Siddhartha realizes that desire is the source of suffering and that by ending desire, suffering will cease. Tradition says that this moment of awakening was prepared for by virtuous living over eons of former lifetimes and came only after he defeated an army of evil demons seeking to prevent his realization.

Seven weeks later, the now-awakened Buddha enters the city of Banaras, meets five ascetics he had previously known, and preaches his first sermon containing "the four noble truths." They are, in their simplest form: first, all life is suffering; second, all suffering is caused by craving and desire and other emotions that drive us to cling to things that are inevitably transitory and constantly changing; third, suffering would therefore cease if we could stop that craving and clinging; and fourth, there is a path that can extinguish craving and therefore suffering. It is called "the noble eight-fold path" and is often divided into three categories. The first is *ethical living;* the second is *meditation* that leads to insight into the ultimate impermanence of all things that we might desire and seek to hold onto; the truth of that insight is *wisdom,* the third dimension of the eight-fold path. The final result of the practice of the noble eight-fold path is detachment from craving and desire and so entering a state where suffering ceases, a state called "nirvana."

After Siddhartha's death at the age of eighty, Buddhism continued to develop as a religion. It appears that early Buddhism was characterized by an almost exclusive emphasis on meditation carried out by a spiritual elite who devoted themselves entirely to the practice of mindfulness in their pursuit of detachment and nirvana. Of course in many Southeast Asian countries into which this austere Buddhism first came, it was complemented in the villages by a variety of folk religions that included divinations, worship of various spiritual powers, and a close-knit communal life.

Such an antimetaphysical attitude combined with an individualistic meditational practice limited to a monastic few did not remain the defining feature of Buddhism. And from the beginning there were complex and beautiful liturgical and devotional practices centering on the Awakened One. Also, early Buddhism depended on beliefs about past lives and reincarnation in which one's present life was seen as the result of previous lifetimes. In addition, the Buddha himself apparently taught that no objects existed independently, but rather that everything exists only as part of a continually shifting network of causes and effects. These interrelations generate the illusion of a substantive reality. The idea of substantial existence is a mistake. Nothing is permanent. Nothing is worth holding onto. This is the "emptiness" of all things including the self.

Thus the tendency in early Buddhism is to dismantle the idea that there are any substantial or permanently real objects. This is in the service of liberation from suffering. If there is nothing substantial, there is nothing to crave. If craving ends, then so will suffering. Centuries of ongoing Buddhist reflection on the meaning of "emptiness" ("shunyata") continually produced new devotional and philosophical treatises throughout Asia, including the famous "Heart Sutra," which proclaims that "form is emptiness; emptiness is form."

In committing themselves to the Buddhist path, Buddhists "take refuge" in the "three jewels": the Buddha, the dharma (the teaching of the Buddha), and the sangha (the Buddhist community). But what does it mean to take refuge in the Buddha? Traditional texts say the Buddha died at the age of eighty. How can he now be an object of refuge? Over hundreds of years, this question generated thousands of answers. Traditional accounts say that when he died, the Buddha asked to be cremated and that his ashes and other relics be distributed to the countries where his teachings had spread. Throughout India and Southeast Asia, these relics were enshrined in reliquaries called stupas. The Buddha was also worshipped in paintings and statues. These Buddhist relics, icons, and other devotional objects soon became incorporated into elaborate rituals. At first, part of taking refuge in the Buddha meant making pilgrimages to venerate the relics and icons of the Buddha.

The more philosophically inclined continued to wonder what was the true object of all this devotion. It seemed to center on the physical body and image of Siddhartha. But the physical body of the Buddha was clearly a part of the physical world and, like everything else in the world, finite and transitory, subject to death and decay. Hardly a fit object for devotion. So speculation arose about other "bodies" the Buddha might possess.

Besides his physical nature, the awakened Buddha also possessed obvious transcendental and eternal qualities (also called "dharma"): his wisdom, his foreknowledge, his infinite compassion, and so on. In typical Buddhist fashion, these were soon made into a list of eighteen "uncontaminated qualities" that were understood to reside in a "body of uncontaminated qualities." So the "body of the Buddha" came to mean less the physical form of Siddhartha and more a list of eternal, abstract qualities, called the "dharmakaya" ("dharma" referring here to these qualities and "kaya" being the Sanskrit term for "body").

The early traditions also contained stories of miraculous journeys that the Buddha took during his lifetime. For example, he was said to have traveled to the celestial abode of his mother, who had died shortly after he was born. For this trip the Buddha was said to use a special body projected out of pure thought called the "mind-made body." These ideas became formalized as the doctrine of the three bodies of the Buddha: his physical body, which he assumed for his earthly life; his mind-made or emanation body, which he could use to take on other forms of life in other times and places; and his body of uncontaminated qualities or dharmakaya.

As time went on, the dharmakaya became virtually a cosmic principle, an ultimate reality in its own right, pervasive throughout the cosmos and manifest in the various Buddhas as they come to earth. A shift in emphasis has taken place here. At first the Buddha was understood as a man who manifested the eighteen uncontaminated qualities. Later he was recognized as the earthly expression of an ultimate principle, the "Body of uncontaminated qualities." It may not be too much of a stretch to say that the Buddha was an incarnation of the dharmakaya much as (we shall see shortly) Jesus was an incarnation of the Logos.

There is a tendency in some secularized Western discussions of Buddhism to downplay the hagiographic aspects of the story of the Buddha and to treat him as simply a wise man who came upon profound philosophical and psychological insights. As the Buddhist scholar Paul Williams says, "Such a model is, I think, misleading. The Buddha was never simply a human being, and is not seen this way by any Buddhist tradition. He always embodies our three dimensions—physical, spiritual . . . , and magical. If after the Buddha's death interest shifts from the physical to the spiritual and the magical . . . this is only natural and embodies a change in emphasis rather than a growing falsification" (Williams, 169). We shall see shortly some examples of this process of increasing emphasis within Buddhism on the spiritual and the magical. And we will find exactly the same process in reference to the life of Jesus and the development of Christianity.

Accounts disagree about exactly when Jesus of Nazareth, who was to become known as the "Christ" (which means "Anointed One"), was born. The early Christian texts tell us little about his childhood. There is general agreement that he was born around the beginning of the common era to a poor, working-class family in a rural part of Palestine at a time when Palestine was suffering severe oppression and economic dislocation as part of the Roman Empire. And that he was steeped in the traditions of Judaism, with its belief in one sovereign God, its claim to be the special chosen people of the one God, and its expectation of a coming Deliverer or Messiah who would overthrow the hated Roman Empire and establish a kingdom of justice and righteousness in its place.

Traditions surround his birth with miraculous stories including that astrologers came from foreign lands and told his parents that he was destined to be a king and offered him gifts symbolic of royalty. Jesus himself appears on the scene around the age of thirty, proclaiming that the "Kingdom of God [an ambiguous term that scholars have argued over for centuries] was at hand." He healed the sick and broke many of the taboos of Judaism by eating with people considered unclean and by teaching and healing on the Sabbath Day when no work was supposed to be done. He associated himself with the marginal and the dispossessed, taught the immediate presence of the Kingdom of God, and gathered an increasingly large following. Thus he appeared threatening to the rulers of Palestine and the Roman authorities they represented. After only two or three years of public life, he was given an imperial execution by the Roman authorities—an excruciating and humiliating public death by crucifixion. No doubt the authorities thought that was the end of the matter.

Three days later his followers were back in the town squares and rural countryside insisting that God had brought Jesus back to life, thus demonstrating that he was, indeed, the long-awaited Messiah. They also claimed that his power and presence now resided with them under the title of the Holy Spirit. They formed themselves into close-knit communities that met in homes and underground locations, meeting for times of teaching and worship that now centered on Jesus himself, taking care of each other, and gradually spreading their "Gospel" (which means "Good News" in Greek) across the known world.

The nascent Christian movement suffered intermittent and occasionally harsh persecution on the part of the Roman Empire, and almost all the early leaders were themselves executed by the Roman authorities. Nevertheless the movement expanded from an underground sect of Palestinian Judaism into a religion in its own right. Diffusing itself throughout the ancient Greco-Roman world, fewer and fewer Christians came from Jewish backgrounds, more and more spoke Greek. Jesus was understood less and less in the Hebraic category of the Messianic Deliverer who would usher in the rule of God at the end of history, and more and more in the cosmic categories common in the larger Hellenistic world.

Already in the earliest documents of the Christian movement, the Christ is being described in more cosmic terms. Twenty or thirty years after Jesus' death, Paul, the movement's first theologian and most active missionary, writes of the Christ that "in him all things were created. . . . Everything was created through him and for him. He is before all things and in him all things hold together . . . he is the origin . . . that he might be everywhere supreme." Later another document, certainly in the Pauline tradition but probably not from Paul himself, speaks of the purposes of God as revealed in Christ as "the uniting of all things together in him, things of heaven and things of earth," and describes the Christ as "the fullness of him who fills everything."

The text known as the Gospel of John begins with the most stunning proclamation of this cosmic Christ:

In the beginning was the Logos
The Logos was in the presence of God
And the Logos was God.
This one was present with God from the beginning
Through him all things came to exist
Without him not one thing came into existence
In him was life
The life that enlightens humankind.

To those who received him
And believed in his name
He gave the power to become children of God
And they were born not of blood,
Nor of the flesh's will,
Nor of a man's will
But of God.

And the Logos became flesh
And made his home among us.

What is the "Logos"? It is a common Greek philosophical term for the most fundamental and universal source of everything that exists. The Logos refers to the cosmic spiritual power pervading the physical world by whose operations the universe is held together, given structure, and governed. Greek philosophers taught that "seeds" of this Logos were sown throughout the world, especially in human consciousness. Thus the human mind participates in the Logos, in the divine reality, and the Logos seeds can, potentially, illuminate human consciousness.

The earliest Christians saw Jesus of Nazareth as the "enfleshing" of this universal cosmic mind. Participating in his life gives the power to become children of God who are born not of flesh but of the spirit of God. There is an ambiguity in the Gospel of John. This phrase, "born not of blood, nor of the flesh's will, nor of a man's will, but of God" could easily apply to Jesus, but here it applies to those who share in his life. This ambiguity makes the point that through joining their lives to his, Christians come to be as he was.

This tradition of our becoming like Christ and sharing his divine life continued throughout Christian history. In the early church, the theologian Irenaeus said that "he became like us that we might become like him." In the Roman Catholic Mass, as he mixes the water and the wine, the priest prays that "through the mingling of this water and this wine may we come to share in the divinity of him who came to share our humanity." On the Sunday after Christmas, the Episcopal Church prays "Grant that we may share in the divine life of him who humbled himself to share our humanity."

The New Testament image of Jesus as the "enfleshment" of the world's universal spiritual source is taken up in Christian thought during the first two or three centuries. One of the first to do so was a philosopher named Justin (later called Justin the Martyr because of his death in the Roman amphitheater in the middle of the second Christian century). A secular philosopher who converted to Christianity as an adult, Justin was familiar with the Logos and other concepts of Greek philosophy.

Justin's understanding of the world (common to all in the second century) involved a transcendental divine reality beyond all human categorization; the physical universe; and an intermediate spiritual reality immanent within the physical world itself (the Logos or "world-soul"). Such a schema admirably fit Justin's goal of translating Christianity into the language of his day. The God whom Jesus called "Father" was the transcendental, ineffable, eternal, uncreated, and nameless source of everything that exists, a unique and ultimate reality and the final goal of our religious quest. The mediator between this unknowable Source and the finite world was the Logos, which the Gospel of John had already identified with Jesus.

Such a schema was adopted with various modifications throughout the second and third centuries by Christian theologians who came after Justin. Irenaeus, for example, who lived in the second half of the second Christian century, also emphasizes the transcendental unknowablity of God the Father. Beyond limits, the divine reality embraces the created order and so transcends it. God contains all things, encompasses all things, and all things participate in God. The Logos—enfleshed in Jesus—is the immanent creative power within the world who "guides and arranges all things." The

Christ then expresses the universal ordering and harmonizing wisdom at work throughout the world.

Thus both Buddhism and Christianity begin with a wandering teacher who gathers a band of followers. The births of both founders are surrounded with miraculous and supernatural events. After their deaths, both are recognized as more than simply mortal.

There are significant differences, of course. The Buddha is described as refusing to talk about God, whereas Jesus had a lot to say about the One he referred to as "Father." At its inception Buddhism begins from the teachings of the Buddha. Christianity originates from an event—the resurrection of Jesus—however that event is understood, and from a particular kind of religious experience that the early Christians called being filled with the Holy Spirit. Early Buddhism primarily advocates a life of wisdom and insight achieved through disciplined practices. Early Christianity evokes a life filled with the Holy Spirit and "partaking in the powers of the age to come."

However, a similar course of development took place in the history of both Christianity and Buddhism. Both the Buddha and the Christ were immediately venerated as objects of prayer and devotion. Following them led their disciples beyond moral and ascetical practices alone to acknowledge a universal spiritual truth. Within decades, each was seen as the expression and incarnation of a universal principle. The ministry of each came to be regarded as an event of cosmic significance. Devotion to the Awakened One or the Anointed One led the devotee beyond Siddhartha or Jesus to a connection to an absolute spiritual reality.

Two Trajectories of Devotion

Consider for a moment the differences between Christian and Buddhist iconography. The Buddha has spent centuries in cross-legged serenity, eyes closed, attention fixed inward, ready at any moment to slip into the contemplative oblivion of nirvana. All life is suffering, begins the Buddha's catechism, and the goal of all right action is to escape its grip. For uncounted millions of devotees, the virtually oblivious Buddha has symbolized the goal of their most fervent quest—the transcendence of the finite and transitory world of woe (called "samsara") through a titanic movement of inward detachment.

For just a few centuries less, Jesus has hung contorted upon his cross. "And the Logos became flesh," says the oft-quoted Christian text, referring to this man of sorrows in all of his tear-stricken, pain-racked fleshiness. For yet other millions of devotees this broken figure has symbolized the essence of the Absolute—a love that empties itself eternally to embrace a suffering humanity.

On the surface, the cross-legged Buddha and the cross-stricken Christ suggest two radically different spiritual trajectories. The awakened Buddha cuts through the veil of pain with a piercing analysis of the human situation and leaves it behind. In an opposite movement, the humble Jesus is said to leave behind the transcendent world of deity and willingly immerse himself in the valley of death. Central in Buddhism is the doctrine of detachment by which the disciple follows in his master's path by learning to dis-identify with the attachments that constitute the finite self and to dwell contemplatively in that interior place that transcends the traumatic transitoriness of mortal life. Central to Christianity is the doctrine of the Incarnation, in which the divine essence willingly attaches herself to the kaleidoscope of consciousness that is human personhood and comes to experience the cruelties and joys of a finite existence. For Siddhartha's followers, suffering was the human predicament and salvation consisted in transcending it. For Christianity, a moral and ontological abyss between God and humankind was the dilemma, and salvation came through a tormented savior who willingly bridged it with an infinite embrace of the sorrows of finitude. What looked like the problem to Buddhism looked like the solution to Christianity.

A story may illustrate these two responses to the problem of suffering.

Miriam (not her real name) appeared in my office as a disheveled shadow of a twenty-five-year-old woman. Long dark hair virtually obscured her features as she hunched herself in my stiffest chair. She strained to whisper out her story as I strained to hear it: a saga of failed relationships, talents as a writer and singer atrophying, and moody black-holes in her consciousness that threatened to devour her. Tremendous native ability and a supportive small college faculty enabled her to earn a B.A. in creative writing but, thrust out into the impersonal ethos of mid-twentieth-century America, she could bring with her only a string of dead-end and deadly clerical jobs. With her face to the wall and her back to me she described the affective darkness that had crept over her life in the last few months. No, she was not on drugs. Her general practitioner had prescribed antidepressants, but they made her sick and so she had thrown them away. And, besides, she didn't believe in medication. Yes, she was able to eat, sleep, and get up and go to work. Yes, she occasionally thought of suicide but was afraid of physical pain (in contrast to emotional pain, which she virtually regarded as her closest friend) and had no real idea of how one who did not believe in drugs might painlessly kill herself.

Gradually the anatomy of her moods was laid bare: an ever-tightening circle of gloom, recently punctuated by periods of rage in which she would throw clothes or books against the paneled walls of her apartment until she collapsed in exhaustion. The proverbial middle child, tightly sandwiched between a hard-driving older sister (now an attorney) and a charming brother (now a corporate trainee), she remembered always feeling on the outside of the family circle. Acting and writing brought her friends in high school and college but, with a couple of exceptions, they had moved beyond the rim of her contact. Casual, brotherly boyfriends in high school and college had been the staple of her social life; she could hardly remember the last time she had gone out on a date. All this activity had kept her moods at bay, but in the last six months their tempo had dramatically increased until she found herself in these psychic black-holes several times a week. After three weeks of description, in which her literary gifts were amply displayed, she asked if I had enough information. I had to admit to myself that I probably did. Now was the therapeutic day of reckoning; how was I to respond to these storms of feeling that swept over the interior desert of her life?

Such raging affections might be regarded as inevitable components of an unstable world, Miriam's depression as the overattachment of the ego to the products of this transitory existence. Therapy might then consist in training her consciousness to detach itself from these phantoms from the world of becoming. There are several reports in the literature of the use of Buddhist techniques of "mindfulness" meditation in therapy with precisely this goal in mind. Mindfulness meditation, as we mentioned earlier, trains the mind to simply observe whatever contents are passing through one's consciousness. The meditator simply comments to herself, "a feeling of pain," or "a memory from my past," or "a sense of joy," or whatever. No attempt is made to change these cognitions, but only to observe them in an increasingly detached manner. The goal is to strengthen what Arthur Deikman calls the "observing self," by developing the capacity to look at one's self from a distance. As this progresses, people cease identifying themselves with their thoughts and feelings, and these mental contents lose their power.

Miriam might be taught the practice of mindfulness meditation, starting with commenting on simple objects in her environment and passing thoughts in her mind. As her ability improved, she might use it in relation to the sea of feelings pounding against her mind and, hopefully, be able to stand back from it rather than drown in it. Here Miriam is trained to distance herself from her feelings so that she eventually masters them through disciplined detachment; it is a transformation through transcendence.

Or, her tempestuous moods might be understood as essential parts of her self, her life, and her personal history that she might engage with, even make friends with, and from whom she might have much to learn. Gestalt schools of psychotherapy envision emotions not as quasi-illusory products of the interaction of a fluctuating world and an attached ego but as manifestations of lost parts of oneself with whom one ought to be reunited. Here the emphasis is on terms such as "awareness" and "contact," and the goal is to immerse the mind in a fountain of feeling.

Miriam might be forcefully confronted with her affections and their every expression in gesture, phrase, or image encouraged and exaggerated; her every attempt to turn from them challenged. With contact established and awareness heightened, Miriam is in a position to discover how furious she remains, even after all these years, about her position in the family and how she still takes their ignoring rejection on herself by holding herself responsible. Only after realizing this with a painful vividness is she really in a position to choose against them. Here the therapeutic trajectory is to go more deeply within the contents of consciousness, to embrace them, dwell within them, and finally come to love and accept them as parts of oneself, despite the afflictions they bring. The gestalt maxim is that nothing is changed unless it is first accepted; it is a transformation by incarnation.

The iconographic images described at the beginning of this chapter exaggerate the differences between Christianity and Buddhism. After centuries of meditating on the detached Master, Buddhism (at least the Mahayana school) enlarged its doctrine by the addition of the figure of the Bodhisattva. Bodhisattvas are those beings who, about to slip into nirvana, return again to this valley of pain in order to aid in the liberation of others. Rather than simply escaping into nirvana, Bodhisattvas re-enter the suffering world to provide assistance to those seeking enlightenment. The Bodhisattva can assume whatever form is necessary to reach a suffering person. While ensconced in heaven, the Bodhisattva remains in contact with those trapped in the earthy realm, ready to come to their aid. From her store of merit, accumulated over thousands of lifetimes on the Bodhisattva path, she can provide grace and protection to all who call upon her.

For example, the next Buddha is already well on the way to Buddhahood. This is the Bodhisattva Maitreya, who is said to be preparing to come to earth in the future to establish a millennial kingdom of peace and harmony. In this guise, he has inspired apocalyptic movements throughout Asia. Until then, Maitreya comes to earth occasionally in various guises to aid and teach. The most popular celestial Bodhisattva in Buddhist lands is Avolokitesvana. He (or she) is said to be continually ready and waiting to save those who call upon him and rescue them from all hardships and perils. He appears on earth as a scholar to teach scholars, as a monk to train monks, as a householder to instruct householders. In Asia, Avolokitesvana is primarily known in her feminine form as Kuan-yin, worshipped throughout the Asian world as the most accessible and caring celestial being.

The Lotus Sutra describes a Bodhisattva called "non-disparaging" because he refused to disparage even the most hostile or dishonest person. Rather he greeted everyone he met with an affirmation of their potential Buddhahood. This ceaseless unconditional love brought him only abuse. Yet he continued to bear all the affliction heaped upon him and, at his death, was received as a Bodhisattva. He is the Buddhist version of the "suffering servant" describe in the book of Isaiah and used as a model for Jesus throughout the New Testament.

Thus within Buddhism the stark trajectory of detachment comes to be complemented by a movement of compassionate return and the embrace of the non-awakened by the awakened.

Likewise the historical and liturgical sequence at the core of Christianity does not end with the torments of that Friday that generations of Christians have come to call "Good." Having drunk the cup of samsara to the bottom and taken to himself that final degradation of the human spirit—death—Jesus arises from the tomb and returns to the heavenly realm from which he came to become the transcendental Lord of Glory so favored in modern Christian iconography. Thus the incarnational embrace of suffering ends in ascension.

In Christianity and Buddhism, the lives of Jesus and Siddhartha are taken as paradigmatic of the journey of the believer. Both lives reveal not a linear movement of either incarnation or transcendence but rather a more subtle and cyclical motion of attachment and detachment. Such a pattern might be discerned in all of life, psychological as well as spiritual. For example, some developmental psychologists portray the early development of selfhood as involving the establishment of a secure bond with the parents, leaving it to venture briefly on one's own, and then returning to the parental embrace. Psychologically and physically (due to the recently gained skills of locomotion), the young self toddles away from its mother. Then the fear of separation is conquered by a temporary return to the security of the mother. Eventually the child can rely on resources within herself to cope with life's inevitable separations.

This process of going forth and returning continues throughout life. We break free of the womb of childhood not in order to fall into atomistic isolation but rather for the sake of the more profound unions and reunions to come. Going from the world of individual development to the universe as a whole, the philosopher Plotinus saw the entire cosmos as constituted by a process of going out from the Source and returning to it. Between the childhood processes described by psychologists and the cosmic processes portrayed by Plotinus, most of us live our lives within a dialectic that involves both attachment and detachment. Our separations are often precursors to higher order reunions; our attachments, when internalized, carry within themselves the seeds of new journeyings forth.

In addition, paradoxically, one can only really separate from what one has first been attached to. Jesus' ascension back to heaven comes only after his Incarnation. The Buddha seeks for the serenity of nirvana only after he has been shocked into identification with human illness, frailty, and death. If the infant is forced into premature separation from the mother, he never leaves the mother behind but rather carries her around as an unsatisfied longing within. And, one can only really identify with what one is partially separated from. The transcendental Christ can choose to embrace humanity. The enlightened Bodhisattva can freely return to earth. Without distance, attachment becomes a fusing loss of self.

Likewise the psychotherapeutic process involves an oscillation between attachment and detachment. Attempts at transcending parts of oneself before they have been accepted, explored, and integrated can lead not to transformation but to a denial in which these unwanted parts of the self do not disappear but rather lie in wait to wound from behind. I recently saw a couple who had left therapy two years before because they had "turned their problems over to God and he [sic] was taking care of them." The brittle truce they had lived under for two years shattered when the wife suddenly exploded at the husband, listing all the things he had done wrong in the past two years, and the husband struck her, and she had the police evict him. Their attempt to prematurely transcend their experience without first embracing and coming to terms with it ended in a bitter disaster.

On the other hand, intense encounters with powerful emotions cannot become ends in themselves, lest like Narcissus one becomes entranced by one's own psychic depths and drowns in them. It is, I gather, part of the wisdom of clinical judgment to know when the client might be guided into a more intense wrestling with the inhabitants of his interior life and when he should be encouraged to transcend them. Spiritualities and therapies of transcendence alone run the risk of a hollow and short-lived victory over interior forces. Spiritualities and therapies of immersion alone run the risk of drowning in the pool of Narcissus.

Miriam waits patiently, almost passively, for her treatment to begin. Through the idiosyncratic dialectic of support and confrontation that we fashion between us, she gains the strength to face, imagine, and dialogue with the demons within her. Thus tamed, they speak to her of the guilt and isolation of her past. Thus she comes to learn that these terror-filled thoughts and feelings are not inborn, like the color of her hair, but rather are the products of her mind's interaction with a rejecting and punitive environment. What was once learned can, if brought out in the open, be relearned. This is a transformation by encounter. And what cannot be relearned can be placed in a larger context. Spiritual disciplines increasingly sensitized Miriam to the existence of more encompassing realities beyond herself, thus broadening her perspective on her thoughts and feelings and allowing her to reposition in a new context those aspects of herself that would not yield to our combined therapeutic efforts: pain transmuted into empathy for others, a sense of estrangement became the basis for a critical distance on life, aggression was tamed into a drive for self-expression, a need for support grew into a love for community. When last heard from, Miriam was working in the publicity department of a small college.

So what looked at first like a difference between Christianity and Buddhism—one embodying a moral trajectory of embracing experience and the other a moral trajectory of transcending experience—turns out rather to be complementary emphases on different sides of a common spiritual movement. Siddhartha went from the painful identification with a dead man, a sick man, and an old man to a search that culminated in the bliss of nirvana and then back to bring his message to a suffering humanity. The celestial Bodhisattva, on the threshold of Buddhahood, remains available to a seeking and suffering humanity. Jesus touched the lepers and embraced the sick and ate with the poor and then withdrew into the wilderness alone to pray and then returned to teach again. The fully lived spiritual life involves times of bliss and transcendence and times of embrace and incarnation. Thus we live out the Buddhist saying that "Samsara is nirvana and nirvana is samsara."

Emptiness and God

I have left till the end of this chapter the issue that, in my experience, always gets raised first when Buddhism and Christianity are compared: the issue of theism versus atheism, with Buddhism cast in the role of the atheist. The Buddha is reported to have said, "I do not teach the existence of God, I do not teach the non-existence of God. I teach the reality of suffering and the way beyond suffering."

As part of this project, the Buddha himself apparently taught that no objects are "self-existing," but rather that everything is only one part of a continually shifting network of causes and effects. This was called "conditioned origination." The universe was understood as an interacting system kept in existence only by the continual interrelations of its parts. These interrelations generate the illusion of a substantive reality. In truth, though, all things are "empty." Thus the "Heart Sutra" proclaims that "form is emptiness ("shunyata"); emptiness is form." And there are the perplexing dialectics of the Indian Buddhist philosopher and mystic Nagarjuna (who, according to tradition, lived from approximately 150 to 250 of the common era), who insists that "Nirvana [and by implication all reality] is not a thing and not a nonthing."

What is the point of these impossibly paradoxical statements? Nagarjuna founded a school usually referred to as "The Middle Way" or "The Central Way" because it seeks a middle way between those who say that emptiness is just nothingness and those who make emptiness sound like an existing Absolute reality. Nagarjuna and his followers are insistent upon avoiding the extremes of either making shunyata simply a metaphysical black hole in which everything disappears or a positively existing ultimate reality. If shunyata were an absolute nothingness, it could only manifest itself as negation. It could not manifest itself as wisdom and compassion. On the other hand, if it were a positively existing ground of being, it could easily become an object of attachment, and so liberation from all attachments would be impossible.

If shunyata and nirvana simply represent an absolute black hole, totally swallowing up the relative, finite world, then entering nirvana or experiencing shunyata would mean totally leaving behind the relative world. Another implication of this would be that ethical action is ultimately meaningless, since it is ultimately empty. However, the point stressed in the Central Way is that "emptiness is not nothingness, and must never be confused with it" (Thurman, 113). Saying that "form is emptiness; emptiness is form," and that "samsara is nirvana and nirvana is samsara" means that the Absolute contains the relative, finite world and the relative, finite world contains the Absolute. Thus the Absolute can be found within the relative world, through human experience and action, sacred texts, and sacramental objects, for example.

There are three realities in play here: the Absolute (nirvana and shunyata); the relative, finite world in which we currently live; and the relationship between them. Wisdom means not only insight into the Absolute and the relative but also insight into the relationship between them. Wisdom involves neither totally separating them nor collapsing them all together (by saying, for example, "they are all just empty"). Form is emptiness, but it is not merely emptiness; emptiness is form, but it is not simply form. "Those who do not discern the difference between these two realities," Nagarjuna writes, "do not understand the profound essence of the doctrine of the Buddha" (Williams, 69). The relative is not absorbed into the Absolute, nor is the Absolute simply a projection of the relative. The integration of samsara and nirvana cannot be achieved by "collapsing either one into the other. The central way is harmonious balance and intuitive wisdom is the non-dual integration of both in equilibrium" (Thurman, 170).

This is the Buddhist doctrine of two levels of truth: the absolute truth and the realm of conventional truth. The absolute truth is shunyata, emptiness. The conventional truth is that the world is real in a literal way. The Buddhist refuses to play these off against each other: either using the doctrine of shunyata to deny any reality to the conventional world, or using the existence of a conventional, physical world to deny the existence of an Absolute realm. Wisdom consists in affirming both the Absolute and the conventional in the way appropriate to each: denying neither the conventional world in which we live or the ultimate reality that is the goal of our practice.

The unity of the Absolute and the relative is not an undifferentiated soup in which all distinctions disappear, but rather a unity in which diversity is preserved. As the Tibetan Buddhist scholar Robert Thurman puts it, "Nonduality is not a unity, a monistic absolutism, and it is not a chaotic plurality, a spiritually nihilistic relativism" (Thurman, 160). It is said that a great Tibetan sage (Tsong Khapa) became enlightened when he read from a classical Buddhist text that "the self is not the same as the aggregates, and the self is not different from the aggregates" (Thurman, 85). As Thurman summarizes this position, "the balance of the central way can be further expressed as an ability to embrace simultaneously objective existence and objective nonexistence, in integrated compassion and wisdom" (Thurman, 170).

We live our lives currently in conventional reality. That is where we seek wisdom and attempt to live ethically. If ordinary reality was simply transitory or illusory or empty of significance, spiritual disciplines and ethical actions done there would be ultimately meaningless. Why seek compassion if it is ultimately empty? Why seek liberation and nirvana if they are simply a void? Such a view of shunyata as emptying conventional reality would destroy Buddhism and undermine the goals of compassion and liberation. The everyday world must be affirmed, for it is the place in which liberation is achieved. But it must also be understood for what it really is—a conventional world arising from ordinary habits of mind; not an inherently existing world.

In speaking about nirvana, the Buddha taught, "monks, there exists something that is unborn, unmade, uncreated, unconditioned. Monks, if there were not an unborn, unmade, uncreated, unconditioned, then there would be no way to indicate how to escape from the born, made, created, and conditioned" (Kessler, 123). The Absolute that lures us forward into enlightenment and liberation is real. The liberation and the enlightenment we gain through our spiritual disciplines are real. They are still regarded as empty. But, remember, that emptiness is not simply an annihilating metaphysical black hole. Writes Thurman, "Clearly enlightenment is not presented as dwelling in the experience of obliteration. Wisdom's diamond drill penetrates the apparent nothingness as inexorably as it does the apparent somethingness" (169). The Buddhist is not saying there is no ultimate reality; she is saying that the Ultimate is beyond "nothingness" and "somethingness"; beyond existing and non-existing. That is, there is an Absolute but it cannot be said to exist in the terms described by finite language, nor can the Absolute be reified or expressed in concepts. The history of Buddhism is replete with examples of this chronic misunderstanding of Nagarjuna's position as equating emptiness with non-existence (see, for example, Williams, 70–71). However, the point stressed in the Central Way is, as we said before, that "emptiness is not nothingness, and must never be confused with it" (Thurman, 113).

Living in the conventional, finite world, we must use our conventional, finite concepts in order to communicate—even to communicate about our spiritual practices and the insights we gain from them. The point of paradoxical writings like the Heart Sutra and the sayings of Nagarjuna is not to deny us the ability to speak. Rather it is to make us aware of the limits of our language. When the Buddhist says there is "no self" or the self is "empty," she is not denying our everyday experience of ourselves as conscious, moral agents. For Nagarjuna words are not descriptions or pictures but conventional tools used to perform tasks in specific contexts. There's no essence of a chair pointed to by the word "chair." "Chair" is simply a conventional expression to aid in social communication. The term "person" does not refer to an essential something that is or is not this or that; it is simply a conventional term to aid in our communication.

The teaching about emptiness is not that nothing exists or that there are no tables or chairs or other people. To the followers of the Central Way, the Doctrine of Dependent Origination means that there is no substantial or inherent existence; not that there is no existence at all. The teaching is not that tables, chairs, other people, and we ourselves do not exist; only that they and we do not exist as we usually think we do. The Buddhist is opposing any reification of language that supposedly refers to some essential or absolute character. By talking about shunyata, the Buddhist is not claiming that things possess something called emptiness. The point is that things do not possess something called self-existence. You may ask, Well, if things do not possess self-existence, what do they possess? The answer is that they do not possess anything.

Ironically I think part of the point of all this intellectual discussion is to put an end to intellectual discussion. Shunyata, nirvana, and the ultimate nature of reality cannot be understood by analysis and reflection. They cannot be understood at all. They can only be contemplated. Such contemplation can, however, result in insight into the nature of reality and in personal transformation. Rational analysis cannot comprehend the ultimate, but when used in conjunction with contemplative discipline it can bring us to the point of what Thurman calls "nonconceptual realization" (Thurman, 55). "Emptiness" is not a concept to debate. It is a contemplative strategy to produce enlightenment. To be fruitful, any reflection on shunyata must be undertaken as a spiritual practice. Its goal must be morally and personally transformative and not simply speculative or intellectual. As Nagarjuna says, "one who adopts emptiness as a viewpoint is pronounced incurable" (Thurman, 153).

Nagarjuna's relentless and single-minded insistence upon "emptiness" proved unstable. In the subsequent history of Buddhism it proved too easy to identify Nagarjuna's dialectics with a nihilistic denial of all truth that, in turn, undermined all spiritual practice and ethical living. Starting from meditative experience rather than from philosophical analysis (as Nagarjuna had done), later Buddhist teachers began to reflect on the ways experience appears in meditation. Sitting in meditation and attending to the stream of consciousness brings home the ways in which our experience is shaped by where we focus our attention and the categories we bring to our experiences. In other words, meditation shows us the ways in which our states of consciousness influence the realities that we can perceive and therefore can know. This is true in every field. After I have studied physics and mastered its categories, I will experience the sun setting differently than if I watch it after having just read and absorbed the nature poetry of Walt Whitman. After studying diagnosis and practicing it under supervision, I see connections between a patient's fever, swelling, and breathing difficulties that appeared simply random and unrelated before. Training my consciousness through immersion in a new discipline enables me to see new things and see old things in a new way.

Consciousness is always present in any moment of insight or knowing. The most objective study of consciousness still takes place within the field of consciousness. Even the most technologically sophisticated contemporary scientific studies of consciousness do not stand outside of consciousness and study it from the outside, but rather study consciousness from within the sphere of consciousness. As long as we are living, seeking human beings, we cannot escape the reality of consciousness. It is presupposed in every path of understanding. It is the final basis of every claim to understanding that we make. Even the insight that all reality is "empty" is not empty of consciousness. Consciousness pervades all the reality we know.

A group of Buddhist teachers took as their starting point this realization that our states of consciousness are always present and shape whatever we experience. Their main teacher was named Asanga and he lived two or three centuries after Nagarjuna. The meditative insight—that consciousness pervades all the reality we know—is taken as a pointer to the nature of Reality itself. Reality in its largest sense was understood as an expression of consciousness. Thus this system is often called the "Mind-only" school. The problem with this title is that it makes the school sound like an abstract philosophical system rather than a path to transformation based upon a meditative practice.

These teachers agree with Nagarjuna that our knowledge of reality is constructed. But rather than dismantle the categories out of which our knowledge is constructed, they focus on the mental processes through which this construction takes place. Ordinary objects are given the illusion of self-existence through the actions of our minds. Once we recognize this, we gain insight into the "emptiness" of ordinary reality and its lack of inherent reality. Thus there is nothing in ordinary reality that we should cling to or try to hold onto. And so we uproot the roots of suffering.

At that same moment, we gain insight into another reality—the power of our minds to shape what we experience. At the core of what we call "mind" is the awareness of the mind's activity in creating our awareness. This awareness-generating consciousness is thus perceived as *the* foundation of all our understanding. This insight into the creative power of consciousness and the inseparability of consciousness from what we know, the inseparability of subject and object, is the transcendental experience of a reality beyond the subject-object duality, beyond any conceptualizations. It is the radiant source of the world as we ordinarily know it. It is called "the realization of the absolutely accomplished," it is enlightenment, nirvana.

This nondual consciousness does exist. It is empty of the illusion that there is a real distinction between the knowing subject's mind and the objects that it knows. But it is not empty in the sense of being unreal. It can even be said that this nondualistic consciousness exists inherently or necessarily, unlike the objects in our ordinary world that exist only in a dependent and impermanent way (Williams, 87). After meditative discipline has pushed us beyond the boundaries of our ordinary awareness, "there remains a really existing, pure, non-conceptual, non-dual flow of awareness"—this essential core of consciousness is the world's true and fundamental reality (Williams, 90).

All followers of the Middle Way subscribe to a teaching about "The Three wheels of the Dharma (the teachings)." The first "Wheel of the Dharma" is the Buddha's basic teaching on samsara and nirvana and liberation from suffering through disciplined mindfulness and detachment. Such a teaching assumes the literal existence of objects and so is suitable for the more concrete-minded disciples. The second turning of the Wheel of the Dharma emphasizes the doctrine of the absolute emptiness of all things. Such a teaching frees us from attachments and ignorance but is dangerous if interpreted too literally and nihilistically. The third and ultimate teaching is "The Middle Way." It teaches an Absolute reality (shunyata) beyond "nothingness and somethingness," beyond being and nonbeing.

Both the strict followers of Nagarjuna and members of the Mind-only school are representatives of the Middle Way of Buddhist philosophy. The strict followers of Najarjuna tend to see the Mind-only tradition as too positive in its affirmation of the reality of consciousness. The members of the Mind-only school tend to see the followers of Nagarjuna as too nihilistic in their single-minded focus on emptiness. Both groups are seeking to find the Middle Way between those who insist that nothing is ultimately real (so why then act morally or seek nirvana?) and those who naively affirm that something Absolute exists in such a way that we can grasp it or cling to it (and so fall prey to the attachment that leads to suffering). Both groups combine meditative practice with philosophical analysis. For both groups philosophical analysis alone leads to sterile intellectualism; it can only lead to transformation when combined with a disciplined spiritual practice.

The Bodies of the Buddha and the Body of Christ

We have already described the development of the doctrine of the three bodies of the Buddha: his physical body, which he assumed for his earthly life; his mind-made or emanation body, which he could use to take on other forms of life in other times and places; and his body of uncontaminated qualities or dharmakaya. The dharmakaya became an ultimate reality in its own right, pervasive throughout the cosmos and manifest in the various Buddhas as they come to earth.

In addition, in the Mahayana tradition the wisdom expressed in the Buddha's enlightenment itself became another cosmic principle called "the perfection of wisdom ("prajnaparamita"—literally, "wisdom that has gone beyond"). The term "prajnaparamita" is feminine in Sanskrit and so the "perfection of wisdom" was said to have given birth to the Buddha, like a woman giving birth to a child. Given its feminine form, this wisdom was often personified and worshipped as a goddess.

A similar practice occurred in Intertestamental Judaism and early Christianity. Many Jewish texts written in Greek during the time of the Hellenistic Empire, in between the last of the traditional Hebrew Books and the time of Jesus, speak about the "Wisdom" of God. In Greek, "wisdom" is a feminine noun ("Sophia") and so the Wisdom of God often appears as almost a feminine form of God. In the early development of Christian theology the Wisdom of God ("Sophia") was often identified with the Holy Spirit of God just as (we have seen) the Christ was identified with the Logos. So the Holy Spirit was called "she" in some early manuscripts. For example, a Syriac version of the Christian creed says, in reference to the Holy Spirit, "She spoke through the prophets."

This discussion of the Wisdom that gave birth to the Buddha soon linked up with another line of reasoning that was occurring simultaneously. The question was, what made it possible for Prince Siddhartha, a finite human being caught in the web of ignorance, to become the Awakened One? There must have been some potential for enlightenment within him. And if all people are to strive to become enlightened, that same principle must be present within everyone. This principle was called the "tathagata-garbha." "Tathagata" means "One who has gone on" and is a common title for Buddhas who have reached nirvana. "Garbha" is a Sanskrit word with many meanings, including "womb," "seed," and "essential nature." The tathagatagarbha is thus the essential nature of the Buddha that gives birth to enlightenment. The Tathagatagarbha Sutra proclaims that this "seed of awakening" or potential Buddhahood exists in everyone. Some later Buddhist teachers expanded this claim to include the entire universe so that every object contains the Buddha principle. Thus potential Buddhas are said to be as numerous as the grains of sand by the sea.

All living beings have within them this womb of Buddhahood. Is it only a potential to become enlightened, or is it the real presence of Buddhahood, which is merely obscured through impurity and an ignorance of our true nature? If it is the latter, then we are already enlightened; we are just not aware of it. Enlightenment is not a change of state but rather the removing of impediments and allowing our inherently pure Buddha-nature to appear. Within this set of teachings there are even some sutras that identify the womb of Buddhahood within us as a self. Not an egotistical or self-centered self but rather an eternal, permanent core of universal selfhood. Such teachings explicitly say that the Buddha's doctrine of no self referred to the self-centered ego but not to the true, universal human nature of enlightened Buddhahood present within each of us (Williams, 98–100).

It did not take long for the discussion of the tathagatagarbha to become linked to the discussion of the dharmakaya. The universal and fundamental reality pervading everything that exists is the dharmakaya which is now also the universal Buddha-nature. This dharmakaya-tathagatagarbha is said to be "beginningless, uncreated, unborn, undying, free from death, permanent, steadfast, eternal" (Williams, 101). In addition, the dharmakaya is said to have "the perfection of permanence [or a "transcendent permanence"], the perfection of pleasure [or a "transcendent pleasure"], the perfection of self [or a "transcendent self"], the perfection of purity [or a "transcendent purity"]." And so this Tathagatagarbha Sutra affirms, "Whatever sentient beings see the Dharmakaya of the Tathagata that way, see correctly" (Williams, 102). Thus the dharmakaya and the tathagatagarbha come to refer to the same thing, the essential nature of things. And, under the influence of the Mind-only school, this essential nature comes to be understood as pure, radiant consciousness. It is empty of impurities, but full of the highest virtues of Buddhahood. When the impurities that obscure it are removed, the Buddha qualities will naturally appear.

Such teachings were controversial, especially in Tibet. The schools that stayed closest to Nagarjuna's teachings taught that the doctrines of the dharmakaya and tathagatagarbha were not to be taken so literally. The only doctrine to be taken literally in their eyes was the doctrine of emptiness (which, by definition, cannot be taken literally). They accused their opponents of undermining Buddhism by re-introducing a real self. Other schools found Nagarjuna's approach too close to nihilism and accused the strict followers of Nagarjuna of undermining Buddhism by removing any grounds for moral action or spiritual practice. They insisted that only some real Absolute could serve as the goal of moral action and the motivation for spiritual discipline. Outside of Tibet, the practices of Zen Buddhism, for example, presuppose a real, universal Buddha-nature to be encountered in the depths of selfhood once our captivity to finite reasoning is broken by the severe exercise of zazen meditation.

The idea of the universe as pervaded by the body of the Buddha (the dharmakaya) has its counterpart in the early Christian claim that the universe is the body of Christ. The biblical face of this vision of the physical world is represented by three passages from the New Testament discussed earlier. First, Paul's letter to the Colossians, Chapter One:

> Christ is the image of the invisible God, the first-born of all creation; because in him everything was created . . . everything was created through him and for him. He existed before all things and in him all things are held together. He is the head of the body, the church. He is the origin, the first-born from the dead, so that in all things he might be supreme.

Christ is the cosmic glue that holds the physical universe together. Strikingly, he is imaged as both the origin or source ("arche" in Greek) of the system of nature and the ground of its systemic coherence. That which is most fundamental in the universe is the source of both existence and (according to this passage) unity.

The universe has the form it does, ultimately, because of the presence of Christ within it—the primal and immaterial spring from which matter arises—for it was created in him, through him, and for him. As its fundamental structure, he is the ultimate explanation for the symmetries that create and govern the process that is matter.

In Colossians the phrase "body of Christ" refers both to the community of devotees and to the cosmos. The cosmos is the matrix for a church universal; or, conversely, the present church is potentially a foretaste of what creation will be. Both are the body of Christ—organisms indwelt by his spirit.

This is made clearer in a second text from the New Testament that continues the themes laid out in Colossians. Ephesians, Chapter One:

> God has revealed to us the mystery of the divine plan which is his will and pleasure which he displayed to us in Christ, that when the time was ready the entire cosmos—things in the heaven and things on earth—will be united together in Christ . . . he raised Christ from the dead and put all things in subjection beneath his feet and gave him who is head of all things to the church, his body, which contains the fullness of him who entirely fills the whole universe.

The model here is of the immanent omnipresence of the one who is the integrating force of the universe. God's plan is to bring the universe to complete harmony by filling it with the presence of Christ. In the fourth chapter of Ephesians, it is said that Christ ascended that he might fill all things.

At one level, even now the universe is filled with Christ, for his presence dwelling in the heart of matter is the source of its existence and symmetry. But that presence has not yet brought the entire universe into harmony. Paul writes in Romans, "The creation waits impatiently, eagerly anticipating the revelation of the sons of God for even the creation itself will be set free from its bondage to decay to enjoy the glorious freedom of the children of God."

The universe itself will be transformed, and the spirit will be completely present in and through it. The universe is neither dead nor static, and the continual transmutations of particles and waves, matter and energy, going on in its depths are analogues for the larger pattern of transfiguration taking place in the entire universe, and visible to those who have the eyes to see the secret plan of God's will—bringing all of creation to unity in Christ.

The final relevant passage from the New Testament, central to the theology of the early Church, is the first chapter of John, which we have already discussed:

> In the beginning was the Logos
> The Logos was in the presence of God
> And the Logos was God.
> This one was present with God from the beginning
> Through him all things came to exist
> Without him not one thing came into existence
> In him was life
> The life that enlightens humankind.

The Logos, the basic symmetry that regulates the motion of the entire universe, the fundamental structure on which the universe is patterned, comes to humankind to give access to that reality.

The roots of a vision of the cosmos as the body of Christ go back to the earliest years of Christianity, when the foundations of traditional Christian theology were being laid. Christianity's first theologians saw the world as a living organism whose soul was Christ. Physical reality was the outward expression of the spirit, or spirit was interior ground of matter. Within matter is a generative power that overcomes its inherent tendency toward chaos, transforming brute material into a complex and living system. This transformation by creation is not the end; it points forward to that time when the universe will be entirely reunited with its creator.

The Church's first theologians weave together a vision of matter as a fundamentally spiritual organism constantly pulsating with vitality, continually undergoing patterned transformations. The presence of the Christ animates and holds together the physical system; he is the spiritual domain from which the physical world arises. By becoming man, dying, and rising again—divine spirit transformed into a physical form and then transfigured again into a spiritual body—Jesus reveals the ultimate nature and destiny of the cosmos: spirit transformed into matter at creation, and matter transformed again into a spiritual body at the end. Thus, he is the archetype, the pioneer, the first born from the dead, pointing the way for all of creation to be set free from its bondage to death. He is also the source from which comes a share in that power, which is pre-eminently his by virtue of his being the spiritual ground of the physical energy that constitutes the universe. Christian spirituality is the human process of entering into that experience.

The Logos did not come into existence with Jesus of Nazareth; the Logos is universally present from the beginning. The cosmic Buddha-nature (dharmakaya) transcends its manifestation in the individual Siddhartha, and the cosmic Logos transcends its incarnation in the person of Jesus of Nazareth. The universal dharmakaya is greater than the individual Siddhartha, and the universal Logos is more comprehensive than the individual Jesus as taught by any single Christian tradition. The omnipresent dharmakaya and the omnipresent Logos make enlightenment and life in Christ possible. All human beings have within them a Logos-nature or a Buddha-nature. However, the Logos is actualized very differently in each individual. Awakening to the reality of the Buddha-nature or entering union with Christ means the realization of the truth of the dharmakaya or Logos hidden within us. A realization in which the ordinary, bounded, self-centered ego is surmounted and reconnected with its source in the eternal, all-encompassing Buddha-nature and Christ-nature.

Beyond Theism and Atheism

So the claim that Buddhism is atheistic and antimetaphysical is much too simple. That may have been true of early Buddhism, but only in a very limited sense. Clearly Buddhism's so-called atheism is not analogous to contemporary Western atheism, which is the product of secularism, scientism, and materialism. The Buddha did not reject God but rather took no position on the existence or non-existence of God, choosing instead to focus on the problem of suffering and its cessation. And the Buddha did affirm the reality of spiritual planes of existence and reincarnation. Siddhartha was certainly no modern secularist. And as it developed, Buddhism has evolved several complex metaphysical systems that often involve various spiritual powers and an Absolute Reality. Shunyata—that which is not a thing and not a nonthing—is often at the center of these discussions.

Christianity too contains a tradition that insists that the Ultimate Reality, called God, cannot be reified or conceptualized. The early Christian theologians mentioned earlier, Justin and Irenaeus, as well as most of their early Christian contemporaries, insisted that the primal and creative divine Source—whom Jesus called "Father"—was beyond all finite speech and categories and so was ultimately inexpressible and unknowable by purely rational means. As the source of Existence, the divine reality cannot be said to exist in any ordinary sense. As that which encompasses all reality, the divine cannot be a part of reality. The previous chapter quoted Dionysious, who insisted that God is "beyond being," and "beyond affirmation and negation," and from *The Cloud of Unknowing,* which describes an encounter with divine reality in which images and concepts vanish. In that sense both Buddhism and Christianity contain a similar trajectory away from a sterile, intellectual debate about whether or not an ultimate reality or God exists in a reified or literalistic way and toward a transforming experience of wisdom and liberation. Wisdom is the insight into the limitations and transitory character of the ordinary world and (at least in the case of Christianity and some Buddhist schools) its arising out of and returning to a radiant source. Liberation comes through the gradual transcendence of our individual egoism and our increasing connection to this greater reality.

Some Buddhist-Christian discussions center on the question of theism versus atheism, others attempt to compare the twin Absolutes of God and shunyata. As much as I love philosophical discussions, to me the important task for today is not to compare concepts. The important task is to undertake the same program within Christianity that the Middle Way proposes within Buddhism: avoiding the extremes of absolutism or literalism (which treat God like a table or chair) and relativism (which denies any ultimate reality and basis for ethical action). For too long Christianity has been torn apart by arguments among those who insist on treating God like a finite, physical object ("An all-powerful *male* in the sky"), or as an abstract, intellectual concept ("a cosmic energy system"), and those who proclaim there is no God and the material world is all that exists. Like the followers of the Buddhist Middle Way, Christians today must insist that there is an Ultimate, Divine Reality that undergirds moral action and spiritual practice and is the source of genuine personal transformation; and that such an Ultimate Reality is beyond finite existence and cannot be captured or entombed in any language no matter how pious or traditional. However, such an Ultimate Reality can be experienced and encountered in ways that lead to deeper wisdom and continual moral transformation.

And followers of the Awakened One and the Anointed One must always connect any intellectual discussion to practice. One goal of spiritual practice is to experience ordinary reality aright: to know that ordinary reality is not absolute and is not a proper object of attachment but rather is the object of compassion. The task of philosophy is to open the way for that experience and to provide categories in which to understand and integrate it. But only a disciplined spiritual practice can provide that insight and enliven these intellectual categories.

Awakening, Liberation, and the New Life in Christ

Both Siddhartha and Jesus appear on the scene as teachers of wisdom, and soon they are seen as expressions of a universal cosmic principle, and then their "bodies" come to represent the pervasive spiritual source of the physical world. To take refuge in the Buddha or to belong to the Body of Christ is to link oneself to this immanent, absolute reality. Such a vision provides the philosophical and theological basis for spiritual practices within Buddhism and Christianity. In both traditions, one goal of spiritual practice is to realize the truth about ourselves—that we have within us the eternal, radiant, and absolute truth of the tagathagarbha or the seed of the Logos.

It is grossly oversimplified to reduce the Buddhist-Christian discussion to a simple equation that Western, Christian thought is personalistic and Eastern, Buddhist thought is impersonal or transpersonal. First, one must be clear what one means by "personality." It is far from clear that what Buddhists deny with their doctrine of no-self is the same thing that Christians affirm when they speak of the self that lives in Christ or is accepted by God.

The Mind-only schools of Buddhism organize the discussion of human nature around a distinction between a "true self" or "spiritual self" and a "false self" or "everyday self"—a structure very similar to that often found in classical Christianity. Also the Buddhist doctrine of no-self should not be lifted from its original context. There it does not mean the extinction of all selfhood or the end of consciousness. Rather this doctrine is almost always found in the context of discussions of increasing or sharpening consciousness through meditation, not extinguishing it.

Clearly there are many different interpretations within Christianity of what is meant by the self or soul, or by the claim that "I have died in Christ." In his Letter to the Galatians, Paul writes, "It is no longer I who live but Christ who lives in me." Who is saying this? Paul? Christ? Does this statement point to an experience within Christianity like that found in the Mind-only and Zen schools of Buddhism of overcoming the subject-object dualism? Paul's statement appears to parallel the paradox in Buddhism (especially Zen) of claiming there is no self. For who is having the experience of no-self? Who is making the claim to no-self? In both cases the loss of self is not a loss of consciousness or will. Enlightenment and "being in Christ" are not forms of coma. Clearly Paul and most Zen masters are among the most active and self-possessed of people. Rather, when the self dies, experience continues. In Galatians Paul suggests that such a nondual experience is at the heart of the Christian life.

Traditionally Christianity and Buddhism have both aimed at a surmounting of egotism and its replacement by compassion. But the means have differed. Buddhism has relied on mindfulness training whereby the individual gradually detaches herself from her selfish desires. Christianity has relied on the experience of unconditional love and acceptance in a relationship to God and the community of believers to transform the individual from self-concern to love of others.

As usual, such dichotomizing of the traditions turns out to be overly simplistic. From the beginning Christians have relied on disciplines very similar to mindfulness meditation to facilitate their encounter with the divine love. And contemporary Christians in large numbers have fruitfully embraced Zen and other Buddhist disciplines as part of their Christian life. And the many Mahayana devotions to various Buddhas and Bodhisattvas and Tibetan Guru Yoga create intense personal relationships between the disciples and transcendent spiritual personages. One can hope that out of the Buddhist-Christian encounter might come the discovery of new ways in which spiritual disciplines that train consciousness and intense, personal devotional practices work together in the service of a deeper spiritual life.

CHAPTER FOUR

Christian Spirituality and Modern Society

Spiritual Practice as Cultural Critique

So far we have discussed why it is important to think of Christianity as a spiritual practice. But, why should we, in this day and age, attend to the spiritual dimension of life and cultivate this sense of presence?

As a psychologist, when I attempt to answer a question like that, the first place I look is at the psychological research. Actually there is a growing body of research on the effects of religious practice on mental and physical health. This is a hot topic these days. Such research has interesting things to tell us and I want to briefly review it in terms of three areas: life satisfaction, mental health, and physical health.

Regarding *life satisfaction*, virtually all studies have found a consistent association between religion, defined in various ways, and a sense of personal well-being. Religious practice seems particularly connected to a sense of life as satisfying. This has been found true for African-Americans, whites, and other ethnic groups in the United States. A long-term study involving almost 2,000 middle-aged men and women found that the presence of religious beliefs and attitudes was the best predictor of life satisfaction and a sense of well-being. Another study of over 800 retired persons found that only physical health was more important than religious practice in predicting how well these people coped with the transitions of aging. As a recent survey concluded, "Faith in a supernatural order seems to enhance subjective well-being: Surveys generally show a small but consistent correlation between religiosity and happiness."

Some, like Marx and Freud, might respond that of course religious people are happier, because they are denying reality. But that puts us in a peculiar position. Marx and Freud and others demand that we face reality. But it seems that part of "reality" is that in order to flourish as human beings we need a connection to things that are not a part of "reality" as they defined it. This puts us in a no-win or "double-bind" situation—a point to which we will return shortly.

As for *mental health,* of course, the question of religion's role depends a lot on what one means by mental health. For example, if by mental health you mean the absence of outright psychoses like schizophrenia or paranoid delusions, the answer is clear: There is no demonstrable connection between religion and any psychotic disorder. Period.

For example, studies done on extremely disturbed populations show either no connection between religion and psychopathology or that the more religious are less disturbed. An early study done on disturbed, psychiatric patients in Manhattan showed less impairment among the more religiously active patients. A study of over 1000 people in the New Haven, Connecticut, area found that psychiatric diagnosis and difficulties were "negatively correlated" with religious affiliation and practice, meaning attendance at religious services and other spiritual practices were a significant predictor of the *lack* of psychiatric problems. A comparison of religious involvement of 100 nondisturbed people with 100 psychiatric patients, matching them on social class and family relationships, found the mentally ill to be distinctly less religious, and the more religious to be distinctly less mentally ill. Such studies have been repeated in a variety of settings with a variety of clinical populations. All find that the more religious are less disturbed.

However, these are all correlational studies; that is, they simply show the connections or lack of them between the presence of severe mental illness and the practice of religion. Such studies say nothing about causality. They do not demonstrate that religion causes mental health or protects against mental illness. We'll discuss that later. Perhaps the most disturbed drop out of religious and other activities, so the less disturbed are the ones remaining religiously involved. However, such studies do refute the reverse causality, for if there is no correlation there can be no cause. There is no evidence, anywhere, that religion causes psychopathology or that the severely disturbed are more attracted to religion, however religion is defined.

A second definition of mental health might be the presence or absence of certain emotional states such as worry, guilt, or anxiety. To answer the question of whether or not religion is connected to such emotional conditions, we have to also think about different motivations for religious practice.

Studies show that some people use their religion as a means to get something nonreligious for themselves, such as social acceptability, respectability, or material success, or are involved primarily because it is expected of them as a matter of social convention. For others, their religion is an end in itself, not a means to some other end. Their religion is the organizing principle of their life. Their religion is lived and experienced.

Studies have found that practicing religion for its own sake is associated with lower levels of psychological distress, better adjustment, and less anxiety and depression, even when such factors as social class, educational level, and family relationships as well as medical history are taken account of. On the other hand, people who use their religion as a means to some social or material end are more inclined toward guilt, worry, and anxiety. This line of research suggests that it is not the content of the beliefs that are psychologically most important, but rather the way they are held and used.

We might consider a third definition of mental health: the presence of certain desirable, healthy personality traits such as sense of competency and control, autonomy, and self-esteem. Again, if we define mental health not as the absence of psychiatric disorders or of emotional distress but as the presence of certain positive personality traits, then it depends on the person's religious motivation whether or not it is associated with mental health.

Take the matter of self-esteem, a construct thought to be central to healthy mental functioning. An extensive series of studies comparing Christians to the general population found no significant differences in levels of self-esteem.

More recent studies that have taken the question of motivation into account have gone beyond that general conclusion and have consistently found positive relationships between certain kinds of religious motivation and traits like self-esteem and personal autonomy, and consistently found the absence of these traits connected to other kinds of religious motivation.

From the very traditional to the most liberal forms of Christianity, using a religious practice as a means to a selfish goal is associated with low self-esteem, feelings of powerlessness, feeling little control over life, while the reverse is true of those who practice their religion for its own sake and draw inspiration from it.

Here we can see something of the complexity of factors involved in the relationship between religious practice and mental health and some hints about how being religious can facilitate either higher or lower levels of psychological functioning. Thinking of religion as a way to get something nonspiritual for yourself is associated with a low sense of competency and control over your life, little sense of self-acceptance, and is also associated with traits like prejudice, hostility, and submission to authority. People committed to their religion as a means for spiritual growth and development tend to exhibit relatively high self-esteem and autonomy (however traditional or liberal their religious affiliations), and tend not to display prejudice or the need for authority.

So, if we define mental illness as the presence of a serious psychiatric disorder, there is no evidence that any type of religion is significantly associated with any type of severe mental illness. Rather there is a clear indication that religion is connected with a lack of severe psychiatric disorders. On any measure, the more religious are less disturbed and the more disturbed are less religious. If we define mental illness as the presence of certain negative emotions—guilt, anxiety, worry—then, among religious people, a more self-centered motivation is associated with those unhealthy states; and those who undertake a spiritual discipline for its own sake show significantly less anxiety and depression than the population at large. If we define mental health as the presence of certain positive personality traits, then again the motivation for being religious seems more important than the denomination one belongs to or how liberal or conservative one is. Again, those engaging in their religion for its own sake tend to exhibit these healthy traits while those whose practice is more self-centered do not.

If you define mental health as a state of satisfaction and well-being, then most religions are associated with those feelings. Several studies have found that hopefulness and a sense that life is meaningful are essential to mental and physical well-being and are a major ingredient in a person's resiliency in the face of crisis, illness, and suffering. Studies consistently show that those who are able to draw comfort and meaning from their religion and employ some spiritual discipline regularly have lower levels of psychological distress, better adjustment, and less anxiety and depression, even when their social and economic status and their general health conditions are taken into account.

Likewise, studies that look at factors like age, social class, education, degree of social support, and recent life stresses find that religious involvement is directly correlated with better *physical health,* even when all those other factors are eliminated from consideration. At least in the United States (where most of these studies were done), those who practice their religion are healthier than those who do not, even when all other factors (including physical condition) are controlled for. Virtually every study, on every measure, finds a positive correlation between religion (however defined and measured) and physical health (however defined and measured). On any measure, those who are religious are healthier than those who are not.

A more subtle analysis reveals that when religion is defined and measured in a more nuanced way, and not just in terms of group participation or holding certain beliefs, a clearer picture emerges. Those who gain meaning from their religion and practice it regularly enjoy better overall health than those who use religion instrumentally, as a way of impressing others or as a means to social status.

All of this is connected to a large body of research associated with the work of Anton Antonovsky that suggests that what is called in the literature a sense of coherence is a significant factor in promoting mental and physical health. This sense of coherence is defined as: (1) the experience that the events in one's life make sense and are not totally random or meaningless; (2) that there are projects in one's life worth committing oneself to and things that one values; (3) that there is a meaning and purpose to one's life. As a species we seem to need to know that our life is meaningful and purposeful. Research has shown that a sense of meaning in one's life is associated with more life-satisfaction and better mental and physical well-being. So these religious concepts like hope, meaning, and purpose turn out to be critical for mental and physical health and for psychological resilience and coping.

Of course, many would claim that meaning and purpose in life are not necessarily dependent on religion. This position is often called religious naturalism: atheists too can experience awe and wonder and appreciate the mysteries of the natural world. They can find meaning and purpose in experiencing themselves as part of the cycle of nature and contributing to it through scientific study and ecological activity as well as through working for the betterment of future societies. I am not arguing against their experience. However, as I will describe in a coming chapter, I grew up and was educated in a totally rationalistic world and found that, for me, there was just too much life experience that could not be satisfactorily encompassed there. But I certainly have friends who feel that their lives are sufficiently meaningful and purposeful because of their scientific work, artistic creation, or political and social service. I suspect this is one of the major dividing lines today between those who consider themselves religious and those who do not: those considering themselves religious or spiritual are convinced that all human desire cannot be fulfilled, and all human experience cannot be comprehended, in the material, physical world alone.

Mediating Factors

This question of whether these beneficial effects of spiritual practice really require spirituality points to an issue that health researchers call "mediating factors." We must never forget that correlation is not cause. Most of these studies are basically correlational—comparing different measures of religiosity with different measures of health or illness. Such studies do not demonstrate that religion causes mental or physical health or illness, although some of the prospective studies come close to that. It could well be that people with certain traits or emotional conditions are attracted to certain types of religion. Or a third variable—type of home, upbringing, social-economic status, etc.—generates both a personality state and a religious type. Although again, newer research uses advanced statistical methods that can eliminate most of these nonreligious factors from consideration.

Still, we now come to the question, How might we account for these findings? First we should note the presence of some obvious mediating factors.

Many religious practices (like meditation, centering prayer, contemplative activities) elicit what we earlier called the "relaxation response." As we have seen, this physiological response has been shown to contribute to a reduction in sympathetic nervous-system activity, improved immune system functioning, lower blood pressure and heart rate, and changes in brain waves. All of these relaxation mediated effects contribute significantly to better health.

Religion has also been shown to contribute to reduced involvement in unhealthy behaviors: alcohol abuse, smoking, drug abuse, unsafe sex, suicide attempts, violence-prone behavior, and an unhealthy diet. This is another important mediating factor.

Research has shown that people involved in a religious practice enjoy increased social support, which has increasingly been recognized as playing a significant role in mental and physical health.

As we have stressed, religion also contributes to a sense of coherence and an experience of life as meaningful as well as to a hopeful outlook on life, all of which are associated with better physical and mental health.

In addition there is the interaction effect between mental and physical well-being. People who feel better physically tend to feel better mentally, and less anxiety and depression have been shown to contribute to better physical health, probably through the effect emotional states have on the immune system. To the extent that religion contributes to one, it indirectly contributes to the other. To the extent it contributes independently to both, there may be a potentiating interaction effect.

There is some discussion in the literature about which of these mediating factors are most salient, especially whether social support is more salient than the cognitive-psychological variables of coherence or mood or individual hardiness and coping skills. There is some evidence, for example, that studies of religion and mortality that evaluate more public expressions of religion (i.e., church attendance) show a stronger effect than those that study more private forms of religiosity. If this finding is solid, it would suggest that, at least in the case of mortality, it is the more social dimensions of religion that contribute to longevity. Again, it is not clear that the case of mortality is generalizable to premorbid mental and physical illness. Certainly in stress-related illness, cognitive and behavioral factors have been shown to be very salient. Again, this underscores the point that the way religion and health are conceptualized and measured can determine the connections found and missed.

All of these factors—relaxation response, healthy behaviors, social support, coherence and meaningfulness—which are clearly associated with religious practice but not unique to it, may go far in explaining the positive effects of religion on health. The question remains, Is there some unique contribution of religion above and beyond these widely acknowledged mediators? Before discussing that, we should be clear about exactly what we are asking for. Even if all of the power of religion's positive effects on mental and physical health were accounted for by these variables, that would not necessarily mean that religious practice has no unique role to play in health and well-being. It may be that religion is a particularly powerful source of, say, social support or coherence and hopefulness. There is some evidence that suggests this is true. For example, research on those who survived the trauma of the concentration camps in Nazi Germany found that those who embraced a religion did better than proponents of purely secular ideologies. Likewise with those who experience "post-traumatic growth" after a severe trauma. Here too religion seems particularly salient. So religion may well produce its effects through well-established channels (like social support, healthy lifestyle choices, and a sense of coherence) without necessarily being reducible to them.

However, the question can still be asked: After all these mediating factors have been taken into account, is there an additional effect that is unique to religion, or are all of the results of religious practice accounted for by already established factors? Does religious practice put us in touch with realities or processes that escape the net of current, or even any conceivable, scientific study? Many studies have used advanced statistical techniques to eliminate other variables from consideration and still found that an effect for religion remains. Studies have compared religious and nonreligious patients who have similar risk profiles (smoking, high cholesterol, obesity, etc.) and found even under those conditions there is a beneficial effect for those with a religious practice. Also studies have found that patients with a religious practice or who report the presence of religious experiences in their lives recover more quickly from major surgery and have fewer complications. Even studies of religion and longevity find that the increased longevity found in those who maintain a religious practice cannot be entirely accounted for by these mediating factors. Such studies, which focus on spirituality alone, make it appear that above and beyond its powerful provision of such well-understood health producing factors as healthy lifestyle choices, social support, and relaxation effects, religious practices make a unique contribution to human well-being.

Spiritual Practice and the Practice of Health

Spiritual practice provides us a sense of meaning by connecting our individual selves to something larger, more cosmic and universal, than our individual egos. Not just in theory. Not just an intellectualized affirmation of the claim that, "Oh yes, there must be some God, some cosmic reality." But rather the lived experience that our lives stand in relation to something greater—God, the ceaseless Tao, the all-encompassing Brahma, the universal Buddha nature. All living religions put us in relationship to something greater than ourselves. This standing in relation to something greater or more encompassing is what gives our individual lives meaning and purpose and so has a demonstrable effect on our everyday health and well-being.

What does it mean that there seems to be this positive connection between having a sense of coherence, meaning, purpose, and hope in your life and being less prone to worry, anxiety, and depression, and enjoying better physical health, and being better able to cope with crises?

One thing it means is that we cannot completely separate the physical, the emotional, and the spiritual. Your spiritual practice and your feelings about it may impact not just on your spirit but also on your mind and body. They may well impact on how anxious or depressed you feel, on your stress level, the functioning of your immune system, the level of neuro-transmitters in your brain, and your cardiovascular condition. Taking this seriously would mean that as individuals we must give a much greater importance to cultivating the spiritual life.

Taking account of this research would also mean that those of us who are health-care providers must see medicine and health as possessing a spiritual dimension. Taking this research seriously would also change how our culture understands what it means to be a human being: it would mean that we are more than just biochemical machinery; that we too posses a spiritual dimension.

Research suggests that religious practice contributes to health and well-being in several ways: by promoting a healthy lifestyle (religious people are less likely to abuse drugs or engage in risky sexual behavior), by providing social support, which is well-established in the literature as a major antidote to mental and physical illness, as well as undergirding the more subtle but extremely important psychological variables of hope and meaning and purpose. On the other hand, a secular, materialistic culture erodes the buffering effects of religion not only by weakening religious communities and therefore increasing social isolation (which is associated with high levels of anxiety and depression and ill-health) but also by undercutting religions' claims about the ultimate ground of meaning and hope.

If Christianity (and every religion) is to fully function as a facilitator of human well-being, it must not only provide increased social support through an enhanced sense of congregational community and through pastoral care. Research on the importance of coherence, meaning, and purpose makes clear that Christianity must also communicate to its adherents the divine reality that serves as the basis for hope and meaning, even though this affirmation goes directly against the rationalistic and materialistic ethos of contemporary Western culture.

The Bind of Modern Culture

Here spiritual practice and psychological research combine to question one of the fundamental beliefs of modern culture: that scientific investigation is the one and only path to the truth.

If it is true, as this research suggests, that faith, hope, meaning, and purpose are important for human health and wholeness, we must also recognize that we live in a culture that officially teaches us that they are illusions. The best scientific minds of our age tell us that the universe arose because of the random collision of a few elementary particles; that life arose and *Homo sapiens* evolved because of the chance mating of a few macromolecules; that all that is really real is matter in motion; and that the future is determined by the rule of entropy, in which the universe and everything in it eventually winds down and dies.

Now let me be clear: my point is not to argue against these scientific findings. I have no reason to think they are not true and I have no expertise in physics or molecular biology that would enable me to dispute them. But as a psychologist I can say that such a vision of the universe puts us in a terrible double-bind, and we know that double-binds can make us crazy. On one hand we know from our experience as well as from the research I just mentioned that we need a sense of meaning and a set of values in our lives in order to flourish. Yet we are told that if we want to be rational and realistic, we must deny these desires for meaning and purpose and value and must recognize that they are the products of wishful thinking that is not grounded in reality. We may comfort ourselves temporarily by enjoying artistic and literary creativity or anesthetize indefinitely though drugs, alcohol, watching TV, or going to the mall. But if we want to be in touch with reality, we must renounce the wish for meaning and purpose and value that gives depth and vitality and sustenance to our lives.

Or, we must find a way, without denying the truth of what science teaches, to affirm the reality of the spiritual life, to affirm the reality of hope and meaning and purpose and value in the teeth of a culture whose official ideology denies them any foundation. How we might do that is, of course, the subject for another book. Here I can only point to this cultural double-bind and make one suggestion.

Religion and Science

For both science and spirituality, training and discipline are essential. Understanding any field requires training and practice. Understanding a field of inquiry requires learning how to perform specialized practices: conducting laboratory experiments, doing statistical analysis, interpreting dreams, studying Torah, sitting zazan. If we don't understand a certain concept—curved space, genetic drift, satori, God—it may not be because the term is nonsense but rather because we don't understand its use within a particular field. What are longitude and latitude lines? Well, you can't find the equator scratched on the surface of the South Pacific, but longitude and latitude lines are hardly illusory. With them, trained navigators find their way around the world. Is the universe really made up of massless, spaceless particles or vibrating strings? Such concepts make no sense in our ordinary world, but they are hardly illusions. With the help of such concepts trained physicists make their way around the mathematics of high energy reactions. Does the human spirit stand in relation to a universal source or ground? Not that you can see by looking at the world of tables and chairs, but with such images disciplined Christian and Buddhist meditators make sense of and communicate their insights.

From the whole range of human experience, each field of inquiry selects one specific area for its study and necessarily ignores all others. This selection is made on the basis of the function that particular field is designed to serve. The physicist treats a falling object—even if it is a person jumping from a building—as a calculus problem, because giving a mathematical account of events is what physics is all about. The sociologist sees such a suicide as an example of a larger social pattern, because relating human behavior to its cultural context is the task of sociology. In the same case, the psychologist analyzes the individual's possible motives, because an account of motivation is central to the work of psychology. And the religious seeker is reminded of the transitoriness of life, because avoiding ensnarement in the transitory world is an essential spiritual discipline.

Such selectivity and functional variety require that different fields give us different accounts of the world of our experience. And no single field can claim to give a complete account of any experience. It is no criticism of a field to say that it is incomplete. There is no choice. All fields of inquiry are. If there is a moral to this story, it is what I call "epistemic humility"—being humbly conscious of the limits of all human claims and fields of inquiry. Problems do not come from speaking psychologically, scientifically, or religiously; they come from insisting that psychologically, scientifically, or religiously is the only way to speak.

To argue, as Sigmund Freud and Albert Ellis have done, that religion is inherently irrational is to presuppose a unitary definition of rationality that cannot be supported even from within the empirical sciences. The rationality needed to solve a problem in mechanics is rather different from that employed in constructing multidimensional geometries, and it is different still from the skills needed to interpret the results of an experiment in high energy physics.

Two further examples or analogies. First, a painting. I can give a chemical analysis of the painting, but I can also analyze it historically, aesthetically, or economically. There is not only one way to describe a painting. The trick of understanding is to ask the right question to the appropriate analyst. If I want to know why the painting has faded, I ask a chemist and not an art historian. If I want to know why it is considered great art, I ask a professor of aesthetics and not a chemist. If I want to know why it costs a half-million dollars, I ask a gallery owner. And so on. I can have many different accounts of the same painting. None is the one and only correct account. Each can be correct, but on its own terms.

My second example is a map. In my car I have several maps of the northern part of the state of New Jersey, where I live. If I want to go hiking there, I need a trail map put out by the Appalachian Mountain Club, not an automobile club road map. If I should want to look for mineral deposits I would start with a United States Geological Survey map and not my trail guide. If I want to know where the political boundaries are in that area, a geological survey won't help me much. A map is a useful tool for doing certain things. But the more things I want to do, the more maps I need.

Empirical science is one lens, but not the only lens, through which reality is to be viewed. Indispensably useful in some contexts, empiricism is impotent in others. If I want to know the causal connections between events in the natural world, I should study physics. If I want to know if I have a moral responsibility to the natural world, the equations and models of physics will do me little good; I need religious wisdom and moral philosophy. And if I want to know if there is a divine presence behind the natural world, I need to take up a spiritual practice.

If I want to understand why a billiard ball goes into the corner pocket, there's nothing like Newtonian mechanics. If I want to understand why a child only touches a hot stove once, there's nothing like conditioning theories. But if I want to address the questions of meaning and value and purpose, so essential for human well-being, experimental method will be of little use. If we want to know why Einstein was attracted to mathematical physics, a good psychobiographical account will surely help us. If we want to know if the theory of general relativity is complete, an account of Einstein's childhood will be pretty irrelevant. Likewise, if we want to know why Martin Luther's or Krishnamurti's religious experiences took the forms they did, psychohistorical accounts like those provided by Erik Erikson or Sudah Kakar are very useful. But if we want to know if there is a purpose in life or if forgiveness triumphs over death, the psychology of religious experience is no substitute for religious experience itself.

Thus spiritual practices need not be antithetical to the natural and psychological sciences. *Science does not say that science is the only way to see the world.* Certain scientists may say that. But such a proposition is not the postulate of any science. It is not an empirical proposition that any science has proven true. It is not necessary for the conduct of science, since many eminent scientists have been and are still religious people. Rather it is an act of faith.

Obviously there are many from both psychology and religion who have a stake in making religion and science conflict. And, if one wants to, one can make them conflict by focusing on limited aspects of religion and of science. Freud focused only on the most infantile aspects of religion that he then easily rejected in the name of science and progress. Ellis chooses only the most authoritarian and dogmatic examples of religion to illustrate its irrationality. But both religion and rationality are more complex and multidimensional than Freud or Ellis allow for. You can make psychology and religion conflict, but you do not have to. It's your choice.

Spiritual practice, then, directly challenges one of the fundamental beliefs of contemporary culture: that scientific and technical rationality is the one and only way to understand the world. In the modern age, spirituality involves learning to embrace a variety of different outlooks. It requires seeing the world in more than one way. It means living in the quotidian world of tables and chairs and also sensing a larger, deeper, more encompassing sacred presence. Spirituality, as we said earlier, involves living with a split consciousness, living with two or more levels of awareness. When I want to know the effectiveness of a drug in treating a patient or understand the physical constitution of the natural world, I draw upon my knowledge of scientific theory and research. When I want to experience the ultimate Source from which the world emerges, I begin to meditate. When I struggle with my moral responsibility in the face of massive injustice or new technologies, I consult the traditional teachers of moral wisdom.

Problems come, I think, when one viewpoint (scientific or religious) claims to be the only true method of understanding ourselves and the world. Then we feel there is only one right way to see things. On the other hand, I can live with a plurality of worldviews (scientific and religious) as long as I don't think any single one is the only one.

The Transformation of Desire

In the previous chapter we spoke about how Christian spiritual practice arises out of desire. This is another place where spiritual practice directly challenges the beliefs and practices of our culture. From the early Christian writers giving practical suggestions for transforming our desires, through Saint Augustine's claim that our hearts are restless until they rest in God, to Kierkegaard's suggestion that we are finite creatures with an infinite desire, there has been this thread of desire in Christian spirituality. Our deepest longing is for a reunion with our Source, and it is the task of spiritual practice to connect us to that desire and to facilitate it.

Here again a spiritual practice directly calls into question another of the fundamental assumptions of contemporary culture: that as human beings we can be fully satisfied by simply acquiring more expensive material possessions. A culture of advertising and celebrity runs on the assumption that a totally fulfilled life can be built around acquiring more possessions. To reinforce this assumption on which their own wealth depends, advertisers employ the most sophisticated psychological techniques to condition our allegiance to the marketplace, and the media continually displays examples of luxury for us to identify with and aspire to. And on the daily news we get extensive and detailed information on the stock market and the state of the economic health of the nation, but virtually no information is available on the nation's social and moral health: How many children go to bed hungry? How many high school students attend school in crumbling buildings supplied with out-of-date textbooks? How many people go without even the rudiments of healthcare? Here in ways they probably do not intend, the media make the basic values and assumptions of our culture clearly visible.

The teachings and practices of the world's spiritual traditions agree that such materialistic pursuits, as pleasurable as they can be in the short run, cannot provide lasting fulfillment and long-term pleasure. This claim has been underscored by recent psychological research that comes to the same conclusion: that the single-minded drive for acquisition does not lead to long-term happiness and may actually diminish it.

Gerald is an agent in the entertainment business. He is in his late thirties and has a severe case of Type I, childhood-onset diabetes. Despite this, he regularly works from 7:30 in the morning till 8:00 at night and usually brings work home in the evenings and on weekends. He and his wife, who manages a women's boutique, both drive late model luxury cars. Even though they have no children, they own a large suburban mansion with several acres of land. She enjoys her work but her store barely turns a profit and she admits she is free to enjoy it because her husband's job supplies them with the luxuries she says they need. Gerald's workaholic style is clearly affecting his health and his marriage, but in the course of marital therapy he refuses to change because he is convinced the only way he and his wife can be happy is through increasing his financial success. His wife, while complaining that they have little marital time together (including time for sex, which is apparently why they are childless), is ambivalent about her husband's work habits since she clearly enjoys driving around town in her Jaguar and agrees that the large house and new cars are the means to happiness.

From my own spiritual practices and study of the writings of the world's religious traditions, I know better. And a recent spate of psychological studies reach the same conclusion, that "the relationship between material wealth and happiness is tenuous at best"—a conclusion reached millennia ago by the teachers of the world's great spiritual traditions. Research suggests that once a certain basal level of security and material well-being has been reached, additional wealth adds little if anything to self-reported happiness. Any psychotherapist, especially those who work with couples and families or have a behavior medicine component in their practices, where they treat people with hypertension or gastrointestinal disorders or headaches and insomnia, probably sees many people who are ruining their marital, mental, and physical health by pursuing the illusion that an escalating accumulation of material goodies will increase happiness. The reverse is often closer to the truth.

Why is that? Psychologists cite several reasons why, after certain basic needs are meet, increasing wealth does not lead to increasing happiness. First, expectations rise faster than material success. Someone who makes forty thousand a year might think that if they just made sixty thousand, they would be satisfied. But research suggests that if they got a raise to sixty thousand a year, their desires would also grow and they would then say they need eighty thousand to be satisfied. Also, the media continually pushes us to judge ourselves against others, especially those who have more. This is a very powerful psychological strategy to get us to crave more and more. So even when we have more, there is always someone who has even more, and so we end up feeling dissatisfied and wanting even more. Third, research consistently shows that the satisfactions derived from any object decline over time. The toy that is exciting today is boring by next month. The car that was luxurious enough today is "old hat" in six months. Again, advertising plays on this psychological fact by continually holding up newer and newer toys to buy as soon as the present ones show any sign of getting old.

Research also reveals that many other things besides material goods are necessary for a satisfying life—friends and family, meaningful and interesting work, intellectual stimulation, physical activity, and many others. But time, as we all know, is finite. As more and more time is spent chasing material things, there is less and less time for family and friends, and for the intellectual, artistic, athletic, and spiritual pursuits that are also necessary for human flourishing. In this sense, the culture's addiction to the sole pursuit of material goods may not only fail to lead to happiness but may end by diminishing happiness through its exacerbation of dissatisfaction and its crowding out of all other sources.

Of course, there is no necessary or inevitable opposition between the search for wealth and human happiness. And lacking sufficient food and shelter, a bare subsistence life is often very unhappy. Clearly a certain level of material well-being is a necessary but not sufficient condition for happiness. But for myself I know that now that I have a decent place to live, enough food, and a reasonable means of transportation, nothing I could buy could give me as much pleasure as spending time with those I love, walking by the sea, doing work I enjoy, and trying to become wiser through reading, reflecting, discussing, and the practices of the spiritual life.

One researcher who has thought and written a great deal about the psychology of happiness has said recently,

> Unfortunately, too many institutions have a vested interest in making people believe that buying the right car, the right soft drink, the right watch, the right education will vastly improve their chances of being happy, even if doing it will mortgage their lives. In fact, societies are usually structured so that the majority is led to believe that their well-being depends on being passive and contented. Whether the leadership is in the hands of a priesthood, of a warrior caste, of merchants, or financiers, their interest is to have the rest of the population depend on whatever rewards they have to offer—be it eternal life, security, or material comfort. But if one puts one's faith in being a passive consumer—of products, ideas, or mind-altering drugs—one is likely to be disappointed (M. Csikszentmihalyi, 1999: 826).

Here psychological research and spiritual wisdom coincide in their rejection of the basic premise of much of contemporary culture. However powerful and convincing materialistic advertising is, the experiences evoked through an ongoing spiritual discipline challenge the equation of possessions and happiness that is fundamental to our culture.

Still the all-consuming ego, denizen of the boutique and the shopping mall, is continually shaped and reinforced by a culture whose slogan appears to be "I am what I possess." What psychologists recognize as basic psychological needs for appreciation, affiliation, and achievement are subtly transformed through a cultural sleight of hand into material needs in the presence of which we feel we have less and less choice. Appreciation depends on wearing the right clothes and bringing the proper wine to the party. Affiliation depends on the car you drive and the size of your investment portfolio and where you go on vacation. Achievement will be enhanced by the latest self-help book, the newest designer briefcase, and the smallest and fastest high-tech gadget. We all want to be appreciated, experience social support, have a sense of accomplishment. So quickly are these desires evoked and linked to possessions that we are given no time to wonder if the model year of our car or the complexity of our electronic gear will really bring us fulfillment.

Thus the all-consuming ego comes to lust after newer and newer possessions and require an ever-increasing array of options. Without new toys to buy and new purchases to contemplate, the all-consuming ego feels bereft and empty. I think of a patient who came to her first appointment wearing a t-shirt that said "shop till you drop" and another who drove his family into bankruptcy and divorce because of his need to continually buy new cars, larger televisions, and higher-priced stereos. The woman readily admitted that shopping exhausted her and it was clear the man didn't like to sit still and watch TV or listen to music. But without a steady stream of things to lust after and eventually to purchase, they were slightly disoriented, felt anxious and bored, and became agitated. Also they reported that without new purchases they had nothing to talk about with their neighbors and coworkers. Thus the addiction to consumer goods becomes redefined as the epitome of freedom and self-realization; bondage to possessions is now called the most complete liberation.

Grinding poverty ravishes the body and can shrivel the soul. Such has been the fate of much of humankind for most of its history and is still the fate of the majority of human beings on the earth. But we are now discovering that a surplus of possessions can also ruin the body and anesthetize the soul.

Oftentimes in the past, Christians have addressed the problem of materialism in a moralistic way. They have preached against it with slogans like "money is the root of all evil." Such moralizing has done nothing to slow the avalanche of advertising campaigns, movies, and television shows that proclaim that happiness is to be found in piling up possessions or to transform a culture built around rape and plunder.

Christian and Buddhist spiritual practices address the cultural myth that possessiveness breeds fulfillment at a deeper level. They do not judge or condemn or engender guilt. Rather they relativize the ego and its greediness. They locate the individual ego in a larger context, thereby creating a new relationship to our ego and its wants.

There is nothing immoral about owning a car, dwelling in a house, dressing well. Things are not the problem. The problem comes in our relationship to them: when we idealize them; when we look upon them to bring us a fulfillment it is not theirs to grant; when the pursuit of them crowds out the joys of walking by the ocean, playing with a child, conversing with a friend or a loved-one; when our lust after them devours our ethical sensibilities.

How can we change our relationship to the things that enslave us so that we can own them rather than being possessed by them? Not by hurling jeremiads at others or ourselves. Not by repressing desire. But rather by transforming it. That is one of the tasks of spiritual discipline: the transformation of desire. In this case, the turning of need back into want, thus reversing the trajectory of manipulation going on in our culture in which wants are transformed into necessities, which we feel we cannot live without. Spiritual practices turn these socially constructed needs back into wants over which we can exercise some choice. We can choose to change the channel, analyze the processes of seduction going on in a commercial, know ourselves well enough that the clothes we wear express who we are and not who their manufacturers wish us to think we are. Spiritual practices are not a rejection of economic life but rather a reconfiguration of our relationship to it.

In the traditional religious literature of Christianity, Buddhism, and other religions, this transformation is almost always referred to as the loss or rejection of the self or ego. To contemporary ears, the language of egolessness or selflessness often appears to connote a collapse into passivity and diffusion of one's selfhood. Like most clinicians who work with religious patients, I have often encountered men and women who rationalize their disavowal of appropriate (and sometimes life-saving) assertiveness and action on behalf of themselves or others or ideals that they say they hold by claiming that they are just "letting it be" or "going with the Tao" or "waiting upon God." Thus passivity becomes the goal of the spiritual life and I am reminded of a quip by Lilly Tomlin: "I married my Aikido instructor because I thought he was enlightened. It turned out he was only passive aggressive." Such a disowning of personal power hardly describes the Zen masters I have known. Paul said that he no longer lives but that Christ lives in him. But Paul was among the most active of men.

So I think we must use the language of egolessness very carefully. Another way is to envision the processes of the transformation of desire as the expansion of the capacity for identification and empathy. Here we move from a life centered on the individual ego (the ego to which the cultural manipulators of our time appeal) to a life centered on more encompassing and transcendental sources of values. Our empathy gradually expands to embrace the universe as a whole. Our individual needs and wants are slowly perceived from an enlarged perspective: not only what will benefit me but what might contribute to the plan of God or the liberation of all sentient beings. We neither collapse into passivity nor constantly live in a guilt-ridden struggle to suppress our desires. Nor do we lose our capacity to enjoy a good meal, a well-crafted piece of music, or the pleasures of love. Rather, through ongoing practice, we increasingly embrace more universal ideals and a more cosmic love. From such a place we can be more resistant to the Sirens of merchandising singing to us from the TV and the glossy magazine. We may make different choices about purchases. We may discover sources of fulfillment that do not become obsolete in a month.

By directly challenging two of the assumptions on which our culture is built—that empirical science provides the only valid way to understand the universe and our place in it, and that material possessions alone can bring us lasting fulfillment and satisfaction—taking up a disciplined spiritual practice can be an act of resistance to and critique of contemporary society.

Beyond questioning two of its fundamental convictions, spiritual practices challenge contemporary culture at a deeper level. Psychology suggests that the need to feel secure is one of humanity's most basic motivations. The vicissitudes of life such as sickness, loss, suffering, and especially death threaten our sense of security. The eruption of inexplicable passions, moods, dreams, nightmares, and other ecstasies also threaten any neat and tidy cocoon of security we construct for ourselves.

In premodern times religion was the major source of that necessary security. Buddhism provided its devotees a security grounded in their ability to detach themselves from the vicissitudes of life through disciplined meditation and in the knowledge that they were being watched and guided by legions of celestial Bodhisattvas and Buddhas. Christianity provided its adherents a similar security grounded in the knowledge that behind the vicissitudes of life a larger divine providence was guiding them and that they partook in the Spirit of God that could bring life out of death. Such sensibilities enabled generations of Christians and Buddhists to face sickness, suffering, and death and embrace the inexplicable realms of ecstasy and dream.

Modern culture, having weakened the power of religion, has had to find other ways to provide that needed security. And, we should note in passing, the reverse is also true: when the security systems constructed by modernity weaken, it is natural that people will look to religious sources for the sense of security necessary for human flourishing. Instead of facilitating religious sensibilities, modern culture has dealt with the vicissitudes of life and its ecstatic mysteries by repressing or domesticating them. Spiritual approaches to the contingencies of life have been replaced by technical knowledge and the drive for control. Illnesses are conquered, natural disasters averted, even death may be circumvented by freezing corpses or by banks of replacement parts. Domains of experience that cannot be totally subject to control are explained away: dreams are only neuronal misfirings, ecstatic experiences are brain chemicals gone awry, passion is subsumed into manuals of sexual technique. If any additional bothersome questions—about the meaning of one's life or the values that should guide our decisions—still remain, they can be sidetracked by trips to the mall or by spectacles brought into your home on larger-than-life TV screens or subdued by pharmacology.

Whether the contingencies of life and the questions they raise can ultimately be either repressed or domesticated remains an open question. Each day psychotherapists encounter the return of the repressed threatening to break out: panic attacks over any perceived loss of control; fear in the presence of any inexplicable physical symptom; inability to cope with loss; troubling nightmares and nocturnal questions. And there are always in the background of consciousness, barely hidden behind the spectacles of an entertainment culture, the possibility of a global economic collapse, weapons of mass destruction, ecological catastrophe. Christian and Buddhist spiritual practices (and those of any major world religion) provide a security not dependent upon imposing control everywhere or explaining everything away. Spiritual practitioners need not repress or flee from life's threatening contingencies. Rather disciplined practice enables us to face them and see beyond them.

What Psychology Contributes to Spiritual Practice

So far I have focused on some of the ways that a spiritual practice might enrich and expand the constricted empiricist and materialistic viewpoint of modern culture and so contribute to our health and well-being. Having discussed what spirituality might add to the narrow outlook of modern culture, at the end of this chapter I want to say a little about what I think modern thought, especially modern psychology, adds to traditional spiritual wisdom.

There are two things that I think contemporary psychology adds to the spiritual wisdom of the great traditions like Christianity and Buddhism: a developmental perspective, and a sensitivity to the ways in which psychological conflicts contaminate the spiritual quest.

First, a developmental perspective. The stage of life at which one enters a spiritual path is important. It is different to take up meditation at twenty, when the search for identity predominates, or at forty, when one is in the process of looking back and reworking a portion of one's life, or at eighty, when one is seeking to come to terms with the course one's life has taken. A conversion experience at fifteen, when the faculty of critical reason is just beginning, is different from a conversion at fifty, when one has, hopefully, developed a larger perspective on oneself. There are important ways that spiritual practices are different depending on the person's developmental stage.

Toward the end of high school, Mark underwent a dramatic conversion at a concert of contemporary Christian music sponsored by a church in his town that he had attended at the urging of friends. The son of an accountant and an attorney, Mark spent most of high school feeling he could never live up to his parents' expectations nor match their successes. He dabbled at soccer, poetry writing, and the science club, but he could never commit himself vigorously enough to anything to be able to succeed at it. Instead he floundered. That warm spring night under the stars with country-rock songs of Jesus' love echoing in his ears and embraced by the current of fellowship that ran through the assembled, hand-holding group, Mark felt an acceptance he never thought possible. He opened his heart to the experience and, without a second thought, gave his life over to following Jesus. Three years later, away at the state university, the local Christian student fellowship was the center of his world. The support and direction he received there enabled him to complete his studies and become certified as a high school history teacher.

Marilyn was raised in a close-knit community Evangelical church. She thought about becoming a missionary but she inwardly chaffed against the church's restrictions regarding dancing and dating. Still, through four years of college and two additional years of nursing school, she lived at home and attended the church in which she was raised. But when she finally received her nursing certification with a specialty in surgical care, she accepted a job in a large urban hospital several hours from home. She found the anonymity of the city exhilarating and made only a half-hearted effort to find a new church. In fact she lied to her parents in their weekly phone conversations, assuring them she was attending church regularly when, in fact, she only occasionally attended a large, rather liberal, downtown Presbyterian church and was freely dating several physicians and interns and frequently attending dance clubs. She visited her parents' home and church that spring for Easter and after returning to her apartment, she called them and told them honestly that she was no longer attending church regularly. There had been no violent rejection, rather a gradual drifting away.

How is it that Marilyn came to reject the same kind of piety that Mark found life-saving? Their very different religious decisions are partially a function of the different developmental stages at which they began to make choices about their faith. Mark encountered an emotional style of Christianity when he was in the midst of the adolescent struggle for identity and direction and in need of an experience of welcome and unconditional acceptance. Marilyn was in a position to consider her religious options at the beginning of young adulthood, with its concern for becoming one's own person and developing a lifestyle of one's own. From developmental psychology we understand that religious needs and practices change with different developmental stages.

The second thing modern psychology adds to traditional spiritual wisdom is a sensitivity to some of the ways the conflicts of the psyche impact on the spiritual quest. A person with serious narcissistic issues may be attracted to a spiritual path that reinforces them—for example, by giving them an opportunity to claim special insights or powers or call attention to themselves through public displays—and so do mischief later on. Any of us who have been involved in a church or synagogue or ashram knows what havoc the presence of just one borderline personality can wreak on a religious congregation. Any of us with an eye for the antisocial character and style can easily spot the many current examples of how the charming and the seductive play upon the good-hearted and unsuspecting among spiritual seekers. Every tradition in the modern world—from the televangelists of evangelical Protestantism to the pedophiles among Catholic and Protestant clergy through the destruction wrought by unscrupulous Buddhist meditation teachers—has seen the mischief that results when spiritual leaders are overidealized and psychological dynamics ignored.

These glaring examples from the headlines should not be fastened on in such a way that it lets the rest of us off the hook. All of us who are spiritual seekers know how our own disciplines have been contaminated by our suppressed desires, narcissistic needs, fears, and insecurities.

Once we get out of the sanctuary or the meditation hall and into the totality of our lived experience, neither psychological insight nor spiritual wisdom can stand alone. Spiritual disciplines and the wisdom they produce add breadth and depth to the findings of psychology. Psychology adds grounding and realism to the spiritual journey. We are fortunate to live in a time when we have both disciplines, both traditions, to draw upon. It was not always so. But today, spirituality without psychology can too easily be naïve and gullible and psychology without spirituality can be flat, one-dimensional, and fall short of what the pediatrician turned psychoanalyst D. W. Winnicott called "the fully human life."

CHAPTER FIVE

Autobiographical Interlude

The Criticism of Criticism is the Beginning of Religion

The twin themes of this book—that Christian faith is best thought of as a spiritual discipline and that such practices are a powerful cultural critique—are deeply rooted in my personal life history. In this chapter I want to make some of those connections between my ideas and my life experiences more explicit.

I was not raised in any religious tradition. In early adolescence I attended a youth group in the local Protestant church, where many of my friends were members; but it was a social experience more than a religious one. My father came from a Protestant background and my mother was Jewish, and their marriage was predicated on the irrelevance of religion. Secular rationalism was the milieu in which I grew up: religion was not attacked but ignored. Emotional expression was discouraged (even punished) and imagination was suspect. One was to be controlled and reasonable at all times. Order, quiet, and efficiency were to be imposed at all costs. Unfortunately I was an emotional kid and the basis for a lifetime of conflict was laid early.

Conflict that, in adolescence, spilled over into the wider community. I attended a junior high school outside of Detroit, Michigan, where seventh and eight graders often carried knives and homemade guns to school. I know this

is all too common now, but it was not in the fifties. I was expelled for strik-
ing back at a teacher who was attempting to discipline me physically in the
classroom, not the first time I was in trouble in school. After that I was sent
to a strict private academy that was supposed to straighten me out. There I
encountered, for the first time, stimulating and challenging classes. I threw
myself into schoolwork. I made the honor role. Boredom in school, I
thought, was the cause of my earlier problems. Now that I was doing well
academically, I thought my problems were over.

That was naïve on my part. Looking back I can see signs that problems
remained, signs that nobody, including myself, paid attention to. The tension with my parents was still there, perhaps more subdued as more of my
energy went into my studies, but still there in periodic eruptions over my
taste in music, friends, and my continual protest against their restrictions.
And I continued to see old friends from my former school. When I got my
driver's license I joined a club that built and raced cars.

I lived two lives: the studious young scholar reading every book on history or science I could find, staying after school to work in the chemistry lab,
and leading the debate team; and, on weekends, drag racing and staying out
late partying. So I learned early to live in many worlds and with multiple
identities: the world of screaming tires and grease under the fingernails and
the world of Cicero and plane geometry; the world of Elvis and Chuck Berry
and Saturday night dates and the world of the local library and the school
chemistry lab; the world of switchblade knives and the world of inter-
scholastic debating contests. Friends died in car or motorcycle accidents and
violence always lurked in the background. Still, since I was doing excep-
tionally well in school, I thought I had settled down.

I was wrong. Taken totally by surprise, I was called into the headmaster's
office in the fall of my junior year and told that "my attitude was not correct"
and I would have to leave. That was the only explanation offered and to this
day I do not know what went wrong. I drove to the local high school that my
friends attended and hung out with them, planning to arrive home at my
usual time as if nothing had happened. As soon as I drove up the driveway
and saw my father's car home early from work, I realized the school had called
my parents. No words can describe the scene that followed. My parents were

clearly exasperated and ready to give up on me and I had given up on them, too. The next morning I packed a few clothes in my car, took all the money I had saved from working since junior high school, and left home. Even after many years of therapy I am still not sure of all that went wrong during that time but looking back, I am struck that as soon as I was able, I left.

After traveling around, working odd jobs, and living in my car for a while, I went to stay with a friend's family in northern Michigan. My friend's father insisted that I call my parents and tell them where I was, which I did. But I was clear that I was not going back there then. I supported myself working in a gasoline station. Having worked summers since junior high school, I had bought an old car and taught myself to repair it, so I was a reasonably good amateur mechanic (this was the fifties in Detroit, after all, and the knowledge of how to fix cars was present in the drinking water).

After a few months of doing this, however, I realized that I did not want to fix cars for the rest of my life. So I took myself on a college tour throughout Michigan, Ohio, and Indiana. In every college I visited I told them honestly that I had no intention of returning to high school. To my surprise, all of them said I should just apply and I would be considered as a regular applicant. So in the early spring I returned to my parents' house to fill out my college applications, gather whatever transcripts and recommendations I could, and prepare to go to college. And so it came to pass that I have two doctoral degrees but no high school diploma.

I felt that colleges were doing me a favor by allowing me to apply without a high school diploma and so I decided to apply only to one, so as not to be in the position of rejecting their acceptance. I chose Earlham College, a small educationally intense Quaker school in Richmond, Indiana. It was absolutely the right choice for me. It combined the academic stimulation I craved with a high level of faculty concern for students that evoked in me a growing sadness that I did not understand or even acknowledge.

It was also a politically active campus and I gravitated immediately to that subgroup. I began college in 1960. Ann Arbor, Michigan, where I had many friends, was close by and I would often return there for discussions featuring Tom Hayden and his cronies and to witness the founding of the Students for a Democratic Society (SDS). And there were continual meetings not only in

Ann Arbor but also in Chicago, New York, and Washington, where the so-called New Left (mostly Midwestern) debated with the more doctrinaire representatives of the Old Left (mostly from New York). Our current turn-of-the-century era of cynicism and materialism makes it impossible to imagine that furious time over thirty years ago, when injustice and the degradation of the poor were causes for outrage, and strong emotions married intellectual intensity and brought forth direct action. I am not one of those who look back on the sixties as a mistake. Just the reverse. I remember it as a time of an exemplary moral seriousness about justice and equality that we could use more of today.

The American Friends Service Committee and the Committee For A Sane Nuclear Policy were continually sponsoring antiwar rallies in Washington, where we regularly confronted senators and representatives over nuclear arms and our government's policies of international torture and subversion in the name of anticommunism. Loyal to the United States, we felt our nation could do better than supply arms to self-serving dictators who used our aid to mutilate their own citizens. Leaders of the burgeoning civil rights movement came regularly to campus to speak. The Highlander Folk School in Tennessee, where the Southern Christian Leadership Conference often held meetings, was an easy drive from Earlham and from there I was quickly recruited to ride integrated buses into the Deep South.

This intense, often angry, political activity was a perfect psychological compromise for me: I could be a bad guy and a good guy simultaneously. I could continue to be angry and confrontive but in the service of a good cause. And through it I maintained a tenuous psychological connection with my family. Like many of my peers in the student movement in the early sixties, I came from a politically progressive family. My father was a lawyer involved in the labor movement and the beginnings of the New Deal. He was close friends with union leaders and other progressive figures in Michigan, and growing up I can remember labor leaders from Africa, Japan, and elsewhere staying at our house. But he rarely talked of his work and after he retired I urged him to tell me about that time or write memoirs, but he refused. And we often disagreed about the confrontational tactics of the SDS and the Student Non-Violent Coordinating Committee (SNCC).

So my political activism represented both a continuity with and rebellion against the ethos of my family. And it revealed something that was going to be a part of my character and style, both personally and intellectually, for most of my life. It is easier for me to define myself overagainst another's position than to simply state my own. Or, to put it differently, I tend to state my own position on something by differentiating it from someone else's. I seem to need that opposition in order to construct a position of my own. This tendency still casts a shadow over my thinking and writing and now I know I have to consciously choose against its pull. And in writing this book I am acutely aware that I experience the spiritual life as standing in opposition to the one-sided materialism and secularism of contemporary Western culture.

I turned eighteen in January of my freshman year. A momentous event for young men of my generation because it meant registering for the draft. The war in Vietnam was just beginning to enter the consciousness of America. In that context I decided to register as a conscientious objector. I had grown up in a violent environment, known violence firsthand, seen friends die, and was skeptical of violence as a solution to anything beyond direct, one-to-one self-defense. Although I was certainly no pacifist, I read everything I could find on the history of Indochina and I knew from the start that that war was wrong and not worth the loss of my life or that of any of my peers. I was helped in this decision by my attendance at a Quaker school and my contacts with the American Friends Service Committee.

Few decisions have haunted me as much as that one. Over the years I have worked with Vietnam veterans and families whose sons (and occasionally daughters) did not come back. I have seen firsthand a little of the way that war ravaged those who "survived" it. All of this has only strengthened my conviction that my original youthful assessment was right. That war was a mistake from the start. On the other hand I've also seen how I was in a position to resist and do the right thing and in the process avoid a price (perhaps the ultimate price) that others paid. I am still tormented by the thought that maybe I too should have gone, or by wondering who went in my place and whether he came back alive. I learned then that no important decision, however right, is free from terrifying ambiguities.

I figured I would devote my life to politics, but after two years of college I realized I was spending more time demonstrating, picketing, and arguing ideology than studying. I felt I was wasting my college opportunity. Also, relations with my parents remained strained and I often spent vacations with friends. When my parents and I were in the same room, the tension over my politics, dress, and attitudes was palpable. The summer after my sophomore year was no exception. I was working in Detroit but all summer the tension grew between my parents and me. We either sat in deadening silence or argued over everything. And the sadness that began when I entered college deepened. Things were happening inside of me that I didn't understand. Toward the end of the summer the tension erupted in an argument (over what, I don't remember) that was so intense that it left me shaken, unable to concentrate or think clearly.

I knew I could not return to college in that condition. I stayed in Detroit, entered psychotherapy for the first of many times, worked in a library, and took a few classes at night at a downtown university. One was a course in logic and philosophy. The professor insisted on using religious beliefs as the butt of all his philosophical argumentation. Whenever he wanted to illustrate a logical fallacy, a mistaken belief, or any other irrationality, he always chose some Judeo-Christian conviction to ridicule. Of course he was egged on in this by a coterie from a conservative Christian student group who tried, and failed, again and again to mount a defense of their cherished beliefs.

I had not thought much about religion since going to college and immersing myself in the world of late night debates over the relevance of Marxism (I didn't have much use for it) and weeklong treks to the nation's capital to petition for an end to nuclear testing or segregation in the South (which I was always up for). Religion played no part in this. I served under the leadership of men from the Southern Christian Leadership Conference but always saw the issues of Jim Crowism in political and legal terms such as justice and fairness, and not in theological or moral ones.

So I sat in that philosophy class and watched this intellectual tennis match from the sidelines. One night it hit me: if the professor subjected his own assumptions to the same scathing criticism to which he was subjecting the beliefs of the hapless students, his would not stand up any better. This was a revelation (perhaps literally) for me. I saw in an instant how his arguments (and all arguments) depend upon beliefs and convictions that he could not prove because they are the basis of any demonstration he could offer. The very formality of logic, with its talk of axioms and primitive propositions, made this crystal clear. Like the proofs of high school geometry that depend upon the acceptance of geometry's axioms, all logical arguments depend upon assumptions that must simply be accepted.

This professorial critic's arguments against belief themselves rested on beliefs. He asserted that his beliefs were obvious and self-evident, but that seemed to me only an assertion of professorial power. His assumptions only looked self-evident because he had accepted a nonreligious, materialistic worldview in advance. His arguments (and perhaps all arguments) suddenly seemed ultimately circular. Later I would come across St. Augustine's statement that we must believe in order to understand and I instantly recognized its truth.

It also seemed to me that the radical empiricism and skepticism of the professor and the dogmatic literalism of the conservative students were two sides of the same coin. They needed each other as foils for their own claims. Each could defend themselves by attacking the other and so relieve themselves of the responsibility of probing more deeply the basis of their own assertions. They could argue and stay locked in this dance of disputation because they shared the same assumption—only literal and concrete statements could be true, whether in science or religion. Although I wasn't aware of it at the time, at that moment began my quest for a way of understanding human understanding that would get beyond that narrow discourse; a quest in which my perennial outsider status and suspicion of authority became an epistemological position, as my oppositional intellectual style was turned against the cultural rule of rationalism in which I had been raised and in which I was being educated.

This realization certainly did not make me a religious believer, but it did make me think I ought to look at religious claims and that it would not be illogical to consider them. In his "Theses on Feuerback," Karl Marx begins by saying, "the criticism of religion is the beginning of criticism" (meaning that any critical analysis of a culture should begin with the culture's religious beliefs). In my experience the reverse was also true: the criticism of criticism was the beginning of religion.

Now the burden of proof was on those who claimed that the reality of time and space was the only reality—a faith that to me could not withstand intense scrutiny. Going beyond rationalistic philosophy was not going beyond reason but only beyond the faith that a narrow rationality is the one and only absolute gate to truth. The paradox of reason was that, carried to its limit, reason reveals its own limits, and by doing so opens up the possibility of a vision of a reality beyond a simplistic rationalism.

Something else was happening simultaneously. Leaving college did not mean leaving political action. I attended antiracism meetings in Detroit and met there a much more radical element of the black movement than I saw in the Southern Christian Leadership Conference. It was my first face-to-face contact with the Black Muslims (who were always polite but unwavering in their assertions) as well as various black separatists and other groups not opposed to violence (or at least to talking about violence). One of the few other white men there was a stocky, balding playwright who turned out to be the Episcopal chaplain at Wayne State University in downtown Detroit—Malcolm Boyd. I began visiting him in his office to talk politics, attending the openings of his plays in small smoky clubs around Detroit, and participating in discussions in his apartment. When my intellectual interest turned to religion, following my realization of the limits of philosophical criticism, Malcolm was there to discuss matters of faith.

He introduced me to the Episcopal Church, explaining its liturgy and doctrine. Friends from school had introduced me to the Roman Catholic chaplain and I began having similar discussions with him. I was also reading everything I could find on the history of Christianity, the Reformation, and the stories of various denominations. Intellectually the Episcopal Church seemed the most attractive: it had the sense of history and tradition and liturgical aesthetics that I appreciated in the Roman Catholic Church. But the authoritarianism and the exclusiveness of the Roman Church, what I regarded as its hang-ups about sex and sexual morality, and its doctrinal and moral rigidity were repellant to me. The Anglican tradition, as I encountered it then, combined a deeply rooted historical foundation with a profound liturgical sensitivity and the greatest degree of intellectual openness and personal freedom. It also had, as I experienced it in both the college chapel and the urban cathedral where I worshipped, a remarkable ethnic and racial diversity. My initial impressions might have been very different if I first encountered the Episcopal Church in one of Detroit's wealthy suburbs or elite preparatory schools.

So before me opened a sensually alive world of candles flickering in the gothic dark, of pungent incense and crystalline chanting, of mystical disciplines that pierced beneath the rigid, empty forms of linear reasoning; A message that "God is love" and "God loved the world," and a thought that love and not calculation or constraint might rule life; A world that touched the inchoate conviction that sustained me through my childhood that there must be more to reality than the cold and bitter rationalism in which I had been raised. I have a friend who is a mathematician, for whom the pure and peaceful forms of pure mathematics brought relief from a life with a hysterical mother and an alcoholic father. My journey has been in the opposite direction. Someone once said that there are two kinds of insanity—the insanity of losing your reason and the insanity of losing everything but your reason. The insanity I grew up with was the latter. And the religious world that valued emotion and evoked imagination promised me liberation from that insanity.

But I was far from sure I wanted to join any church. I was an inveterate loner through high school and even in college. While I always had friends and was never an isolated person, I felt like an outsider in any high school or college group. And I joined various student political causes. But I always thought of these as transitory, pragmatic commitments in order to accomplish goals. Joining a church was much more of a commitment than I could easily make. And churches then (and now) often describe themselves with the metaphor of a family, and that was not a metaphor that had positive associations for me.

And I had been attracted to the "New Left," with its nondoctrinaire and anti-ideological stance and its slogan of participatory democracy. Religious institutions seemed among the most doctrinaire and least participatory on the face of the earth. While I certainly understood that we all need to drive on the same side of the road, authoritarianism of any kind was (and still is) abhorrent to me. And it had been glimpses of personal religious experience—ecstasy evoked and imagination unleashed—and not doctrinal propositions or moral demands that promised liberation from the secular straitjacket of my past. This formative experience continues to shape my understanding of Christianity as centered on experience and practice rather than built upon doctrines or rules.

So I entered a period of intense personal struggle with my fear of joining any organization, especially a church. Mentors like Malcolm and other clergy tried to reassure me that despite the trappings of authority, ironically the Episcopal Church was one of the most open and least authoritarian. That was certainly how I experienced it then, too. And the irony of a church with bishops and cathedrals encouraging freedom of thought was very appealing.

My friend the Catholic chaplain tried to convince me that the post–Vatican II Roman Catholic Church would also be a place where diversity of thought and intellectual freedom would be valued. I was not convinced, and later he left the priesthood with his hope unrealized.

Although I could not articulate it then, I sensed a difference between Anglicanism and the Roman Catholic and Protestant Churches that I encountered then. Historically, it seemed to me, Protestants tried to attain unity by insisting on confessional or doctrinal unity, while the Roman Catholic Church tried to attain unity by submission to authority. My anti-ideological and anti-authoritarian inclinations made both impossible for me. In Anglicanism, as I encountered it back then, unity is maintained not by confessional hegemony or authoritarianism, but by situating oneself in a historical lineage and involving oneself in common liturgical and devotional practices. People of incredibly diverse beliefs and commitments can engage in the same liturgical practices and so stand in the same lineage. And by doing so I could imagine that there might be a place even for someone like myself, who never seemed to belong or fit anywhere. So from the beginning, I experienced the Christian life first and foremost as a set of practices. At first this primarily meant liturgical and devotional practices. Later, in large part through my study of both Buddhism and the spiritual writers of the first Christian centuries, my practice expanded to include various meditative and contemplative disciplines.

But the problem was deeper. Starting with my family, the experience of belonging was so tinctured with pain that just the thought of it was the source of much inner conflict. Some of the conflict took the intellectualized form of debating with myself and others about the role of institutions, about how far I could in good conscience abandon my anti-institutionalism, and about considering the reasons for and against belief. But the conflict also took a more emotional form of sleeplessness and confusion.

Marshalling my sense of being an outsider in order to stand over-against the secular rationalism and empiricism of my familial and academic milieu made it relatively easy to accede to the possibility of a spiritual reality beyond the rim of the empirical universe. And Anglican Christianity with its grand tradition of mystical discipline and evocative liturgical symbols was the obvious carrier of that possibility. And once I had removed the blinders of rationalism (but not of reason), the power of such a possibility kept pulling me forward toward the affirmation of its reality.

The image of the spiritual journey captivated me. Journeys are not destinations. I did have to have fully arrive some place. And I felt the Episcopal Church welcomed those who were still on the journey and had not arrived at a complete understanding of God. I did not understand the doctrine of the Trinity or the substitionary atonement (and I still don't), nor was my life even close to exemplifying the virtues of Victorian morality. But I felt pointed in a direction: I wanted to understand more deeply the inexhaustible mysteries of divine reality and embody more fully the gospel principles of love and forgiveness. At the end of that year I was baptized and confirmed.

And since I wanted to understand the religious form of life more deeply and experience it more intensely, I decided to go to theological seminary. In many ways academic pursuits had been a conflict-free domain for me. Even in high school my studies were the one thing I could devote myself to unreservedly and where I received a modicum of positive reinforcement. Ever since I started college, I had imagined myself being a university professor, since studying and learning new things were one bright spot in my life. Given my interest in religion, I decided to make that the focus of my scholarship. I never imagined myself becoming a parish clergyman but rather a scholar of religion. Fortunately the bishop of Michigan at that time had himself been a professor and he was encouraging of my wish to combine ordination and academics.

In many ways my commitment to Christianity carried an even greater rebellion against and break with my family than did my political activity. SDS and SNCC could be seen as legitimate extensions of the progressive wing of the labor movement and New Deal to which my father was devoted. And on the principles of social democracy and racial equality we agreed completely. But making religion central in my life was a direct repudiation of what I sensed was at the core of my parents' interfaith marriage—the belief that religion was unimportant. And I was committing myself to a way of life so completely different from their own, in which emotion and imagination rather than obsessive reason and technical efficiency were to have major roles. My parents greeted all of this with mixed emotions: on one hand they were glad I finally seemed to have a direction in my life, but the choice of religion as a field of interest perplexed and distressed them.

I returned to Earlham College that September, switching my major from political science to religion. My approach to politics had also changed. Discussions in Malcolm Boyd's apartment with Muslims and separatists and some firsthand exposure to the conditions of blacks in Northern urban cities had chastened my earlier embrace of the moral idealism of Dr. King. Little of the Southern legal Jim Crowism existed in the North, but the conditions for African-Americans were no better and were perhaps worse. I stayed in touch with the civil rights movement but, when the Mississippi Freedom Summer was organized the summer after my senior year in college, I decided not to go South again. And, if my memory is correct, shortly after that summer whites like myself were expelled from SNCC after angry confrontations within the movement.

My first real identity was as a political person. Now that had changed. The relationship between my turn to religion and my disenchantment with politics is complex. Many of my peers made a similar move. After the Mississippi Freedom Summer and the growing fury within the black movement that followed it, and, demoralized by their powerlessness in the face of the escalating irrationality of our government's Vietnam policy, many white students began turning from political action to embrace the new religion of Timothy Leary and LSD. My joining the Episcopal Church and deciding to go to seminary was analogous to this shift in the mid-sixties.

A year in Detroit, away from the endless debating of the student movement and the inspiring rhetoric of the Southern Christian Leadership Conference, opened a space where a deeper questioning of politics began. Looking back I noticed that while "participatory democracy" was the slogan of the student movement and there certainly was a lot of debate, still, major decisions were made and statements written by a few, and hierarchies of more or less committed partisans were falling into place. Not fancying myself a leader, I didn't mind this. But I was also reading history and seeing how revolutions seemed always to devour their offspring and that rarely did much change except the names on the doors and the affiliation of those rotting in prison.

I began to feel that another level of transformation would be required if these dynamics were to be avoided. I remember reading and debating a widely circulated article by Che Guevera in which he maintained that "a new man" (misogyny was far from absent in the New Left) would be produced by new revolutionary social conditions. From what I could learn of the aging revolutionary society in the Soviet Union and the incipient one in Cuba, there was little evidence Che was right. The basic conviction of the New Left was that all problems were at root political. But, in ways that I could not articulate, I was losing faith in that creed. So, from the beginning my commitment to Christianity was tinctured by my oppositional style: my opposition to the one-dimensional, rationalistic milieu in which I grew up; my growing opposition to the faith in political action alone that I had once embraced.

Another thing that had happened to me in Detroit was that I discovered psychotherapy. My therapy with a young psychologist was primarily Rogerian and supportive. But I grew in the support, and the experience of someone listening empathically was powerful. There were few interpretations, and so at the end of the year I understood little of what had happened to me. But in the presence of what D. W. Winnicott would call a "holding environment" I was able to mobilize whatever internal resources for survival had sustained me through early adolescence and gradually return to a functional state.

This experience made such an impression that I decided to minor in psychology and so began my inner dialogue of religion and psychology. Together they had been my major influences during that crucial year in which I had gone from a reactive, angry, and unfocused activist to a committed scholar concentrating on understanding religion. Together their discourses promised precisely the deeper transformation I was missing in the rhetoric of politics.

A provocative undergraduate class in religion and psychology and extended visits to Earlham by two of the preceding generation's major voices in the discussion between religion and psychology—Paul Prusyer and Victor Frankl—reinforced my growing interest. Together psychology and religion consumed all my studies during my final year of college and set the course that has continued to the present.

My embrace of Christianity had been, in keeping with my personality, a rather intellectual thing. I had seen a way out of the prison of rationalism in which I had been raised. Seeing the limits of the totally cognitive and instrumental made thinkable a reality beyond the purely material. But affirming such a possibility was not the same as experiencing or knowing it firsthand. At first I was so relieved to be liberated from that prison and so enchanted by the insights of the new world opening before me that I didn't notice this problem. But it gradually made its presence felt as that year progressed.

As the year progressed, I became increasingly troubled. I went to church regularly and was moved by the music and symbolism. I took classes in religion and was challenged by an entirely new way of thinking in which paradox and complexity were central. I discussed religious issues with every faculty member or classmate I could find. But my lack of firsthand experience cast a deepening shadow.

I became increasingly lethargic, unable to concentrate, and depressed. Intellectual affirmation of a religious possibility was not the same thing as a life-giving religious experience, and the gap between them was slowly swallowing me up. I went to the college infirmary, got checked out, and was discharged, since no organic problem was found. People were full of well-meaning but useless advice: pray, go to church, give up this religious nonsense, get involved in a new cause. None of these suggestions were possible for me. I was in the grip of something and I could not get free. I felt myself sinking into an emotional black-hole where no light shone and from which nothing emerged.

Finally I could fight it no longer. I had no choice but to give into it. One chilly, early spring Midwestern afternoon I gave up and went out into the woods that bordered the Earlham campus to die. Not to commit suicide. I had no intention of taking my own life. But I felt that if I gave into this inexorable drift downward, the flame of life within me would just flicker out.

I sat with my back against a tree and just let the suffocating darkness engulf me. No will to live, no desire to go on, no interest in anything, no life-force left, no resources to mobilize. I have no idea how long I sat there, virtually comatose, barely breathing, unaware of my surroundings, drowning. Certainly it was many hours, for night came down around me and wrapped me in its black embrace.

Suddenly, unexpectedly, from beyond any place I could consciously summon, beyond any expectation I consciously held, a feeling of power raced through me. I was infused with a current of energy that started from where I was sitting and shot through my body. I remember my slumping body jerking upright, my eyes popping open. Even though it was deep night, I could see the outlines of the trees around me. I felt like I had been brought back to life. I remembered words from the Gospel of John about passing from death to life. I felt sustained by an eternal power, stronger than death, that I could hurl myself against the world and I would not ultimately be destroyed.

I jumped up, ran back to campus, knocked on the door of a faculty member I knew well, and tried to tell him what had happened. I doubt I made much sense. He and his wife listened patiently and, since it was late at night, walked me back to my apartment and insisted I get some rest. The next day the sky looked bluer, trees stood out more sharply from their background, classes were more stimulating, ideas more interesting than I ever remembered. And I felt in possession of a genuinely fresh and real knowing.

What happened to this experience?, I ask myself, almost forty years later, as I'm writing this. It propelled me through the process of studying religion, applying to theological seminary, and confirmed my reorientation from a single-minded rationalism and political pragmatism to pursue the spiritual life. But it did not last. It was too overwhelming. I had no context in which to nurture or maintain it. I had learned the difficulties of sustaining a purely intellectual affirmation. Now I also learned the difficulties of (in my case, impossibility of) sustaining a transforming experience by itself. Gradually the immediacy and power of that moment dissipated.

Faint echoes of that earlier experience have gradually returned to my life more recently. Not as a spontaneous eruption of experience but rather as the result of ongoing meditative and contemplative practices. This process of having, losing, and gradually regaining such a transforming sensibility has strengthened my emphasis on spiritual practice. Overwhelming experiences can only be sustained and matured in a context of ongoing spiritual discipline. Without it, they simply dissipate. Neither a purely intellectual faith nor a momentary "peak experience" can develop into a maturing and transforming spirituality without some disciplined practice.

I have seen a similar pattern with patients who were deeply involved in the hallucinogenic world of the late sixties. Many had profoundly moving and potentially transformative experiences back then. But, in my experience, only those who used these "mind-blowing" episodes to spur them to take up some ongoing psycho-spiritual practice benefited from their experiences in terms of increased wisdom and maturity. Others either did serious psychoneurological damage to themselves or left these experiences behind along with their bell-bottom pants and long hair.

At the end of that year (1964) I went off to the Episcopal Theological School and the Harvard Divinity School in Cambridge, Massachusetts. Again I felt like something of a misfit. The theological community was in the process of discovering the civil rights movement and the power of direct political action. Many around me wanted to talk of demonstrations and confrontations, whereas I wanted to learn about prayer and theology and ecclesiastical history. Though supportive, I was fresh from learning the limits of episodic political action after the bitterness of the Mississippi Freedom Summer, the dissension over the role of whites in SNCC, my harsh year of conversation with the armies of Muslims and black nationalists in Detroit, and the spreading disillusionment as the war in Vietnam escalated and younger contemporaries were being snatched away to feed the beast. As classmates went south to march, I applauded, contributed money, and stood on the sidelines. My students now have a rather cynical saying that (I am embarrassed to say) captures my attitude at the time: "Been there, done that."

Through friends I found my way to a house church in Cambridge: a small ecumenical group of Harvard and M.I.T. professors and graduate students, evangelical but not fundamentalist, which became my spiritual home. I took classes at the Episcopal Seminary and the Harvard Divinity School, went to chapel regularly, and worked as a seminarian in a parish on Sundays. I met wonderful people, made good friends, studied with brilliant faculty and soaked up an incredible amount of knowledge about the Anglican tradition. But I was always thinking slightly at cross purposes from these communities. I was just as politically radical as ever in my outlook and commitments, but in my mind I was not there to go on demonstrations or debate public policy but rather to journey deeper into the heart of the divine mystery.

I graduated from seminary in 1967. My interest in religion and psychology remained. So first I decided to do graduate work in religion and then later do additional training in psychology or psychotherapy. So off I went to Brown University for graduate work in religion.

Among students, Vietnam had subsumed all other political concerns. I joined the Brown student movement, but most of the (often endless) meetings were devoted to debate and discussion; people seemed under the illusion that talking about the horrors of the war would really contribute to ending it.

I worked as a draft counselor. I felt a mixture of pity and shock at the rather privileged men of Brown whose lives seemed all mapped out for them and who had reached late adolescence and never had to make a real life decision (I did not consider choosing between Brown and Princeton a real life decision). Now they were faced with a choice that would determine the rest of their lives, and they had no idea how to make it. Rules for conscientious objector status had tightened considerably in the few short years since I had gone through that process. And I felt helpless myself in the face of their stark alternatives: go to war, go to jail, go to Canada. I knew men who chose each of these alternatives. Later I would visit some in jail and others in Canada and later still work with "survivors" of jungle warfare. Every choice shattered (and ended) lives and families. And I was struck by how little sympathy or support these agonized young men received from others in their lives— parents, older faculty, girlfriends. I remember thinking to myself that I was watching the destruction of a whole generation of men.

As an academic and an outsider I was an object of suspicion by the Episcopal Diocese of Rhode Island (the machinations I had to go through to complete the ordination process would fill another book). Finally I found work in an African-American parish in the heart of the Providence ghetto. When Martin Luther King was shot I remember walking through the dark, rubbled streets with the rector—the only two white men in sight—to conduct a memorial service.

The end of the sixties brought chaos to college campuses and to America. Cities I knew well—like Detroit—came to resemble Berlin after the Second World War: here and there a hospital or church remained standing, otherwise it was heaps of cinderblocks and broken glass as far as the eye could see. LSD was making inroads into the minds of my generation and the one directly behind. Cambridge, Massachusetts, looked like the Black Hole of Calcutta, with pale high school students panhandling and passing out on the streets. Stores in Harvard Square sported plywood in the windows instead of glass as a precaution against student rioters. Like its sister schools, Brown was shut down after four of our compatriots were murdered at Kent State.

I watched all this from the sidelines. I did not heed the call from the SDS to go to Chicago in 1968. Instead I watched with a mixture of horror and envy (since I was no longer where the action was) as young men and women just like me with blood pouring from their heads were thrown into police vans, and Tom Hayden and others were summoned to court on trumped-up charges while mayor Daley sneered his way through his address to the Democratic National Convention. I heard rumors of former acquaintances taking lessons in bomb-building and going underground. And I saw more and more emaciated, mind-blown adolescent bodies sleeping in doorways in Harvard Square.

I was hearing a different drummer. Skeptical of the effectiveness of episodic direct action, too self-protective to put holes in my head with LSD, I concentrated on my studies, my parish work in the impoverished core of Providence and later in an equally impoverished rural community to the west of Providence, and doing whatever I could for the young men facing the draft: counseling, visiting them in jail or in Nova Scotia, and sitting with them watching the TV as the draft-lottery randomly consigned some to careers as Wall Street lawyers and others to be compost in Southeast Asia.

At the end of the sixties, the student movement imploded: the Civil Rights Bill had been passed, the lottery ended the draft as a pressing issue, the beatings in Chicago and the deaths at Kent State sent the most radical voices underground or fleeing to Haight-Ashbury. I went to Minnesota to teach religion, and a year later was offered a job at Rutgers University in New Jersey to be involved in the creation of a new department of religion.

Devising two or three courses a semester at Rutgers, hiring faculty and serving as chair of the new department, plus the birth of a daughter, then another, and then a divorce, consumed all my time and energy. My interest in jointly pursuing religion and psychology took a back seat, although I was in therapy again, this time with an analytically oriented psychologist whose interpretive skill began the process of my understanding what had happened to me. But eventually the new department was established, my relationships with my daughters had stabilized, I published a book and was given tenure and the old interest in religion and psychology began to reemerge. I volunteered to work at the college counseling service, took a one-year leave and received further clinical training, and later, in a moment of temporary (I hope temporary) insanity, returned to graduate school to work on a second doctorate in clinical psychology.

I arrived at my graduate studies in psychology in the midst of a debate about the scientific nature of psychology. Some defended the claim that psychology was a science like physics. But their concept of physics was one that no physicist had used for a hundred years; all they could do was listen for the hum of machinery. Others insisted that psychology and the human sciences were a completely different enterprise than physics or chemistry. I listened to this debate from the perspective of someone who had already written two books in the philosophy of science and its relation to the philosophy of religion. And what struck me was that both those who defended the scientific status of psychology and those who rejected it assumed a rather old-fashioned, literalistic viewpoint on the nature of scientific claims—the very viewpoint I had encountered in that first philosophy class and that I had spent my professional life trying to get beyond.

So for three years I was both a faculty member teaching full-time and a graduate student at the same institution. I entered graduate school this second time with a fantasy that I would gain the tools to integrate religion and psychology. I had grandiose visions of a unified field theory, Hegelian in its scope, which would synthesize the disciplines. Years have passed since my classes in psychopathology, statistics, and experimental design. In those years I have learned a new body of theory and research, gained and used more diverse and sophisticated clinical skills, been socialized into another professional identity. And the fantasy of disciplinary integration has gradually evaporated.

Instead of producing a great synthesis of religious and psychological concepts, I learned the importance of practice. Fruitful dialogue between psychology and religion will only grow out of the lived experience of those who have religion and psychology as part of their actual lives; from practitioners, not from uninvolved theoreticians who are only interested in moving concepts around; from those who struggle to live out a spiritual path and are immersed (as therapists, patients, students, or all of the above) in the actual practice of psychological research and treatment; those whose theorizing can be informed by practicing. That is why this book emphasizes the importance of practice in the spiritual search.

I used to get impatient if reading or thinking or dialoguing didn't seem to produce an immediate integration of religion and psychology. But I realized the goal is not, cannot, be some ready-made, instant, shake-and-bake synthesis and integration. The goal is to keep faith with the process of living on that boundary. That is all that is asked, to keep faith with the process. Often people speak of spiritual paths and intellectual journeys and then treat them like they are really destinations, and get frustrated and angry if they don't feel they've arrived yet. Well, in the interaction of psychology and religion, no one has arrived yet. All we can do is hang in there with the process of dialogue. And my hope is that this book can make a contribution to that process.

CHAPTER SIX

Spiritual Selfhood

Spiritual Practices and Everyday Life

Two Approaches to Life

There are two distinct ways of looking at life, and they can be symbolized by the difference between hiking on the Appalachian Trail and white-water canoeing.

When hiking on the Appalachian Trail you have a detailed trail guide put out by the Appalachian Mountain Club. The trail is well-marked with "blazes," colored markers on the trees and rocks. Supposedly the next one can always be seen from the preceding one. The trail is easy to follow. Every turn and every change of direction is indicated by markers and described in detail in the guidebook.

When hiking, you can take your own time. You can stop whenever you want in order to rest or snack or catch your breath or relish the view. You can consult the guidebook and plan ahead exactly how far you will travel each day.

Now, hiking the Appalachian Trail can be very, very, very strenuous. Many times I have felt sick from exhaustion on steep climbs and came close to passing out. I have been caught in unexpected downpours, mudslides, and snow storms. And I have seen how easily a person can get hurt if they are not alert or in decent physical condition or well prepared. But, if you follow the maps and trail guides, you always know where you are and where you are going and how you are going to get there.

White-water canoeing is just the opposite. Currents change without warning. You have little control over your speed and direction. Swift water suddenly gives way to calm stretches. You are gliding leisurely with the current, watching beautiful autumn scenery drift slowly by, thinking that this is all right. Then suddenly you are almost up-ended by unexpected rapids. No guidebook. No blazes or markers. No posted warnings. No well-traveled path, worn down by those who preceded you. You are always thrown back on your resources and those of your companions.

You can never master a river the way you can a trail. Every time you canoe down it, it is subtly or even dramatically different. Mastery is not possible. Coping and developing skillful means of surviving constantly changing currents are the only possibilities.

Many people want the Christian life to be like a hike along the Appalachian Trail. Yes, it can be very strenuous, and storms come up unexpectedly; but the trail is well-marked, you know your destination, and the guidebook is always there to help you. For them, the Bible should be like my old, dog-eared Appalachian Mountain Club guide: telling me in advance of every twist and turn, what provisions to bring, where the dangers lie, and how to avoid them.

As is clear from the previous chapter, you know that my life has not been like that. One of the reasons I enjoy hiking and have only gone white-water canoeing twice in my life is that white-water canoeing feels too much like my everyday life. It is no vacation to feel jostled by unexpected waves, to strike unforeseen submerged obstacles, to be driven along by currents over which I have little control.

With my life, a guidebook is impossible. I am not disappointed or angry with my faith when it fails to produce a well-worn path and a well-marked road through life. I don't expect that from my religion. A guidebook or a triptych through life is not realistic for me or for most people in this fast-paced world. Thrown back on my own resources and those of my companions, what I need are disciplines that develop my inner resources, coping skills I can use when I encounter the unexpected twists and turns of life, and trustworthy companions to travel with.

Listening to students and patients, I sometimes think that people expect their spiritual practices to protect them from the vicissitudes of life. They think spirituality should enable them to rise above the currents and obstacles of life. It should protect them from the catastrophic and the unexpected. So when children or spouses die young, when marriages end, or businesses fail, when the inevitable suffering enters their life, they get angry at God, furious at the church, frustrated with their faith. And they never question whether or not their expectations were realistic to begin with.

I remember when the Roman Catholic Church changed its liturgy from Latin to English. A friend of mine who was a Catholic priest described how, during the first Sunday of the new, English Mass, people threw things at him and called him names while he was saying Mass and afterward cursed him at the door of the church. Many had believed that the Church never changed anything, and became enraged at the Church and the priest when something did change. Of course the liturgy has changed a lot since the time of the Apostles, and it will continue to change in the coming centuries.

I knew a man who was a prominent leader in his church until his wife was murdered in the course of a robbery. He quit the church, bought a gun, and became a bitter and angry person, constantly furious at God and anyone he associated with religion.

In this white-water situation called life, there is no guidebook that will guarantee me a smooth journey. Instead it is who I am—my character, the experiences I've had, the skills I've developed, the knowledge I've gained—that I must rely on. This is what I call my spiritual selfhood—who I am as a moral and spiritual person. When my job is threatened, my marriage ends, someone close to me dies, that is what I have to rely on—my spiritual selfhood.

I don't look to my faith to give me a roadmap or a trail guide to life. Rather I look for it to equip me with the skills I need. It is not realistic for me to feel like I can master life or rise above it, any more than I can master a swiftly flowing and ever-shifting river. It is more realistic to learn to cope, to acquire inner resources, to develop a sense of spiritual selfhood.

Spiritual Selfhood and the Practice of Psychotherapy

My idea about spiritual selfhood grew out of the way in which I think about my work as a psychotherapist. For me, one of the most important things about psychotherapy is the use of self: How do I use myself when I am doing therapy? One of the ways I think we therapists choose techniques of therapy involves how they enable us to use ourselves or how they restrict our use of self.

There are some psychotherapeutic techniques that I could never use on a regular basis because they are so incongruent with who I am; I could never use myself in the way they require. I once had a supervisor who was trained in a very austere style of psychoanalysis. As much as I respected this person's intellect, I once said to him that if he convinced me that was the best way to treat patients, I would give up therapy and go back to being an auto mechanic. With my relational proclivities, I could never, on a regular basis, be that detached. Years ago, when I was in training in family therapy, I watched some of the masters of paradoxical and strategic therapy. As much as I admired their ingenuity, I've probably used techniques like that only once or twice in my life. Although I feel I can learn something from watching anyone who works well in any specific mode of doing therapy, there are many modes of doing therapy that do not work well for me because I cannot use myself in the ways they require.

Without necessarily bringing any specific spiritual techniques into the therapy session itself—teaching patients to meditate or saying a prayer with them (things I do not do)—I think that being a spiritual person, a meditator, a woman or man who prays regularly, a person who communes with the natural world in a disciplined way, shapes the person I am when I am being a therapist, and a teacher, and a citizen.

I am one of those people who think that the most important tool a therapist has is their self—their life experiences, their sense of humor, their empathy and compassion, their intelligence and creativity. Techniques, interventions, and interpretations are important, but they take place in a relational context. Beyond very narrowly defined problems like a single fear of heights or snakes, research suggests that two therapists can use the same technique and get remarkably different results. What the research literature calls "nonspecific factors"—like the quality of the relationship between the therapist and the patient—have been found to play a significant role in how successful or unsuccessful the therapy is. So, preparing the therapist is at least as important as preparing the therapeutic techniques.

I think this is a lesson from the practice of psychotherapy that applies to much of life. In coping with the ever-changing currents and sudden rapids that constitute our ordinary lives, who we are as spiritual persons is at least as important as any bits of information or particular skills we have learned.

So how do spiritual practices help prepare us for everyday life? How do religious disciplines help us develop that spiritual selfhood?

I want to suggest that there are certain experiences basic to our lives, that most (if not all) human beings encounter, that have both psychological and spiritual dimensions. I call them "primal experiences" because they seem so fundamental to human life. Spiritual practices prepare us to deal with them. I give two examples in the following section.

The Primal Experience of Alienation from Self and Source

The first example involves alienation, conflict, or division within ourselves. One of the things that all the religions of the world agree on is that there is something out of joint about our ordinary human life. In other words, all the religions of the world perform what I would call a clinical task—they give a diagnosis and prescription for the human condition. Of course the contents of those diagnoses and prescriptions vary greatly among the various traditions. But all the major religions have this clinical format of diagnosis and prescription.

For Hinduism the problem of life is our ignorance of our true nature, in which we have lost touch with that eternal and universal dimension of ourselves that transcends time and space and joins us to everything else that exists. For Buddhism the problem of life is our clinging attachment to the things in our lives; this clinging inevitably leads to suffering when loss comes, as it eventually always does. For Islam the human problem is our falling short of the divine law. For Christianity the human predicament comes from our lack of conformity to the plan of God. And so on. Every religion offers a diagnosis of the human condition.

What is the relationship between these spiritual and moral diagnoses proffered by the world's religions and the diagnoses given by clinical psychotherapists?

I think it would be naïve and overly simple to suggest that the alienation and suffering pointed to by the great spiritual traditions are the same as those diagnosed by the clinical specialties. But the research that finds that those who hold to some spiritual or religious outlook and are committed to some spiritual practice are less prone to anxiety, depression, and other major and minor psychopathologies suggests that spirituality and psychological health are connected in some way.

This research on the relationship between spirituality and psychological health or pathology should influence how we think about health itself. In most languages the words for mental and physical health also carry connotations of spiritual transformation and well-being. Only in the modern world have we been taught to separate physical and mental health from spiritual well-being. The modern view of health, influenced exclusively by technological medicine, defines it as the absence of symptoms. But is a person healthy simply because they are not depressed or anxious or suffering from some diagnosable condition? Is a person healthy simply because they have no particular reason to call the doctor? Perhaps. But a person may not be depressed or anxious or in physical pain and still find their life devoid of meaning. They may still awaken in the middle of the night with their head full of agitating questions. They may still feel empty as they drive home after a day's work. Such conditions might be called pathologies of the spirit. Such alienation from our full selfhood may cause or exacerbate anxiety, depression, or substance abuse, but it is unlikely to be cured by interventions aimed only at these psychological conditions.

Sometimes Christians and Buddhists and other people committed to a spiritual path suggest that some concerns or conditions (usually labeled as "spiritual") are "higher" or more "advanced." I'm not sure in what sense this is true. A person who is suffering because they are having panic attacks and cannot leave the house is in just as much distress as someone who finds their life empty and devoid of meaning, or is burdened with guilt after a life of self-indulgence and acting out.

Increasingly in my experience, and that of other psychotherapists I know, people come to see a psychologist with these kinds of concerns—concerns that are clearly spiritual or religious in some sense. Formerly most people came with clearly diagnosable complaints that significantly interfered with their daily lives: they were depressed, anxious, had panic attacks, were plagued with obsessions, were always in fights with coworkers, could never hold a job.

In my practice, I still see people with these major syndromes—major depression, anxiety, panic attacks, substance abuse, obsessive behaviors—but increasingly I also see people who are not having any obvious and overt symptoms. They may be functioning very well; they may be very successful on the job; they may socialize openly and confidently. Yet inside they feel empty, disconnected from their work and their family, dead inside.

One such patient—a successful Wall Street trader—described himself as an idea going through life in a three-piece suit. Another, a skilled and respected surgeon, told me he was having more and more trouble just getting up in the morning and going to work. He was not depressed in the usual diagnostic sense, but he said his work had lost its meaning even though he was continually having a profoundly beneficial effect on many peoples' lives through the operations he performed. Or a person comes for vocational counseling and they are given tests to evaluate their interests and abilities. But the real issue turns out to be not discovering their skills and talents but finding what they value enough to commit themselves to.

What is going on here? What is going on is that physical medicine and psychotherapy are sometimes not enough. And I say this as a practicing clinical psychologist. What is going on here is that there is also a spiritual dimension to our lives and if it is ignored the result is just as much pain and suffering as that caused by physical illness or psychological distress. I think that is partly why there is an upsurge of interest on the part of physicians, psychologists, and other health-care people in religious and spiritual issues and their impact on physical and mental healing.

Just as there is a spiritual dimension to our lives, so there is a spiritual dimension to the alienation we experience: an alienation that may show up in the physical and psychological symptoms of stress, depression, substance abuse, emptiness, and anomie. Christianity, like all the major religions of the world, insists on this—that, whether we are conscious of it or not, within us all is the potential to become separated from and ignorant of the spiritual source of meaning and purpose for lives and of values to guide our daily living.

So one primal human experience is this sense of alienation, or estrangement, or falling short of our values, or lacking meaning and purpose to our lives, or doing again and again the things that go against our conscience.

Death and Rebirth

Another primal experience on the boundary between psychology and spirituality is the cycle of death and rebirth. Virtually every religious tradition has some variant of the saying from the New Testament: "unless a seed falls to the ground and dies, it cannot bear fruit." Virtually every religion has said that spiritual growth and transformation involve some dying, some dying to self.

Psychologically this process of dying to self usually involves being pushed to the limit. We can only discover what is beyond the limits of our ordinary life when we are pushed to the limits of that life. The spiritual masters of the early Christian Church called this "resignation." That sounds so grand, but what it really means is giving up, being exhausted, coming to the end of our rope.

Creativity has this same structure. A friend of mine who is a professor of mathematics describes how he wrote his doctoral dissertation. He had labored for months and months over a problem in multidimensional geometry, to no avail. His wife and young daughter were getting anxious about his ever finishing. He was getting impatient with himself. One particularly frustrating day he threw down his pencil and took the laundry to the laundromat. As he was folding the laundry on the table, the solution to his problem suddenly appeared before his eyes. He dropped the laundry (much to his wife's chagrin), ran home, and finished his dissertation in a matter of weeks. It was only when he felt pushed to his limits and gave up his struggling with the problem that the solution appeared.

Among the most powerful examples of this transformation through resignation, of death and rebirth, can be found at meetings of Alcoholics Anonymous. They call it hitting bottom. The alcoholic struggles and struggles against the bottle and the bottle always wins. Finally he or she hits bottom, gives up, comes to the limits of their illusory willpower in the face of their addiction, and only then, in the acknowledgement of their powerlessness, are they open to a "higher power" and the transformation that openness brings.

Such moments of transformation, of dying and being reborn, stand on the boundary between the spiritual and the psychological.

Another example of this process of death and rebirth comes from developmental psychology. Stages of development can be seen as a series of small deaths and rebirths. Often one must give up the stage left behind before one can move ahead.

I remember when one of my daughters turned five. After the party and the gifts, I said to her as I was putting her to bed, "Now that you are five, you will never have to be four again." (I think I was the one who was relieved that she would never be four again.) She immediately broke into tears, demanded that I send all the presents back, and said she always wanted to be four. I'm sure that now that she is an adult and a successful professional woman, she is glad that she did not remain four forever. But I think we all know what she was feeling back then.

Or, the child leaves home and goes off to college and comes back an adult. And happy is the child who, when he or she returns, has parents who welcome them back as an adult. But in order to welcome our returning children home as adults, we parents must first grieve for the end of a certain kind of parent-child relationship. Development too is as much a process of grieving and mourning as a process of growing and maturing. Or, to put it better, any process of growth and development also has elements of loss and grief.

I think this is a place where Christian traditions differ among themselves—or at least appear to differ—in their understanding. Some years ago I was teaching a course in a psychology program run under the auspices of a conservative Evangelical Protestant university. One day one of the students asked me rather confrontively, "Do you Episcopalians believe in redemption?" Of course, I replied, but I think redemption is a process and not a single event. I may have a single powerful transforming experience, but I still live in the world of time and I still have a life-long process of growth, of deepening, of transformation to undergo.

The spiritual directors of early Christianity understood that redemption must enter into our lived experience and that it is an ongoing process of self-knowledge, of dying to rather than clinging to destructive impulses and patterns. They did not expect a kind of shake-and-bake, instant redemption that is fully cooked in an hour. Rather, they looked for a continuous, seesawing, process of transformation; a process facilitated by various spiritual practices like the Jesus Prayer, meditative visualization, morally responsible living, and communal worship.

Spiritual Practice and Spiritual Selfhood

What does all this have to do with the role of spiritual practice in developing a spiritual self? A disciplined spiritual practice puts us in touch with these primal experiences. Spiritual disciplines make us more aware of the depths of our alienation, the strength of our self-centered attachments, the places where we fall short of our ideals, the areas where we remain ignorant and unconscious, the times in which the good we would do we don't and the evil we wouldn't, we do. Such practices also immerse us in the cycle of dying and being reborn: distancing ourselves from our attachments, seeing our conflicts in light of a larger perspective, giving up cherished illusions about ourselves and others, dying to them and mourning for them.

As one sits quietly and meditates, suppressed wishes, fears, and frustrations rise into consciousness. Sitting still, we cannot run from them. We have no choice but to either face them or give up our practice. Here we are brought face to face with the fears and wishes that dwell within us.

Primal experiences such as these are among those repressed by the glitz and glare of contemporary life and the belief that more possessions will quiet them or new drugs suppress them. Awareness of such primal experiences can shake a sense of security based on the equation of possessions with happiness or the illusion of total control. Here spiritual practice moves in the opposite direction from the security operations of contemporary society. Rather than turning away from such apparently threatening experiences, spiritual practice faces them directly. Rather than dulling our consciousness, spiritual practice intensifies our encounter with the vicissitudes of life, and with our moral shortcomings, and with the large and small losses we face daily.

Spiritual practice does not evoke the realities of failure, anxiety, loss, and ultimate death for sake of nihilistic posturing or cynical detachment. Rather, spiritual disciplines give us the audacity to take them upon ourselves: to meet failure with forgiveness, to meet loss with meaning, to meet fear with courage, to meet death with the hope of new life. Thus spiritual practice not only challenges the foundations of contemporary culture but also provides an alternative outlook on life.

Meditative practice also forces us to confront the ways our desires constantly shift—from wanting newer and bigger toys, then on to opportunities to help a friend, then off to seek more intense sources of pleasure, and so on and so on continually. Meditative practice, if we stick to it, quiets our minds and sharpens our powers of self-observation; bringing to light our wishes and our fears; revealing our attachments to things and the egotistical ways we use others. In meditation we scrutinize these buried facets of our personality not in order to criticize or condemn ourselves but rather to see these often hidden parts of ourselves in light of our spiritual commitments. Thus we may develop some detachment from them and desensitization to them. These dark places within us will not disappear, but they have less of an addictive grip on our lives.

In my tradition, every Sunday we reconnect ourselves with a body that was broken and blood that was shed and the renewal of life that they brought forth. Techniques such as visualizing Jesus forgiving the prostitute; or reflecting quietly on enigmatic paradoxes such as having to lose a life in order to gain one, or that form is emptiness and emptiness is form; or surrendering to the embrace of the beauty of the ocean or the majesty of the mountains, can open us to sources of power and insight beyond our conscious and individual selves. Our sorrows and joys thus become part of a larger vision of life.

Spiritual practices like these reconnect us with these primal human experiences of alienation within ourselves and of dying in order to be reborn. Thus spiritual practice prepares us to hang in there with the struggles of our lives (and the lives of others)—to sit with our grief, to empathize with others' struggles and stuck places, to absorb their angry outbursts and be patient with our (and their) difficulties. This is how we grow that spiritual selfhood we need in order to live freely and creatively in the midst of the uncertain waters of everyday life

People often ask me, How can you sit and listen for hours at a time to other people's troubles? Doesn't it drag you down?, they ask. The answer is no. Partly because the intense person-to-person contact of relational psychotherapy, when it is going well, exhilarates rather than drains me. But even more important, the emotional intensity of a patient hitting the bottom of their depression, or owning up to their murderous fantasies, or sinking into the process of mourning a dead relationship—these do not scare me or drain me because the practice of spirituality has long before acquainted me with such primal human experiences and made them familiar, much the way that my personal therapy did. But spiritual practices go beyond personal therapy by relocating these struggles in a larger context that gives them additional meaning.

Spiritual practices relocate and ground the struggles of life (and of psychotherapy) in which alienation is faced, lost opportunities and cherished wishes grieved, hope restored, new life brought to birth. Spiritual practices relocate and ground these processes in the larger, sacred, cosmic truth of transformation and restoration in which we daily pass from life to death and back to life again. Spiritual practices ground these processes in the reality of a power that is at work within the world and within us all to bring life out of death.

I know the patient is not alone—and none of us are alone—in their confrontation with failure, their loss of illusions, their dark nights of the soul. Not only because I am there with them but because saints and gurus and masters from all ages and cultures have gone there before them. And, from the standpoint of Christian belief, such experiences have even been taken up into the very life of God through him who was made like his brothers and sisters in every respect.

I worked for two years, one day a week, in a maximum security prison, and my colleagues on the outside would often ask me, How can you stand to go into that place seething with barely contained violence, and sit in a small unguarded room, face to face with men who had stabbed their brothers, shot their wives, or beaten strangers in the dark? And my answer was hardly original but it was profoundly true. Every time I heard those steel doors clang tightly shut behind me, and I looked around the tiers of cells, I said to myself, "There but for the grace of God go it." Had I faced what many of those men faced, I might well have ended up where they did. Little that is essential separates me from them. As the American psychiatrist Henry Stack Sullivan is reported to have said, "We are all more human than not."

At the conclusion of his collection of moving accounts of his work with patients called *The Fifty-Minute Hour,* the psychoanalyst and novelist Robert Linder (author of the novel *Rebel Without a Cause*) writes, "I know that my chair and the couch are separated only by a thin line. I know it is, after all, but a happier combination of accidents that determines, finally, who shall lie on that couch, and who shall sit behind it." There is something about both the practice of Christian spirituality and the practice of psychotherapy that brings home to me that we are all more human than not. And every time I sit with a patient despairing over the death of his marriage or facing the fact that he is not the person he thought he was or mobilizing herself to take the first step toward the object of her fears, I think to myself, "There but for the grace of God go I," because we are all more human than not.

I am hardly the most disciplined of spiritual practitioners. I tend to be too eclectic and too erratic to make much progress. But from what little I've done I know that the struggles of my patients and my own struggles must be part of a larger, sacred, divine activity by which suffering is transformed and life brought forth from death.

Chapter Seven

The Mirror of God

Coping and Transformation

A s we approach the end, we need to review where we've been. We suggested that the Christian spiritual journey involves alternating times of the felt presence of the divine reality and times of the loss of that sense of presence. The loss of that felt presence need not be a negative event. It does not necessarily herald a loss of faith or the absence of God. Rather it may be the beginning of an experience of a Reality that is beyond all our intellectual categories, beyond time and space, beyond description, that cannot be captured by our ordinary words. Times of the absence of God may begin our initiation into the "Cloud of Unknowing." They may be times when God is calling us to move beyond our ordinary religious symbols to a new experience of God that goes beyond all concepts.

Such experiences, however, rarely happen spontaneously but rather are the result of discipline and practice. Earlier we stressed the importance of practice for understanding and experiencing the Christian life: that learning involves doing and that learning something new involves doing something new. Cultivating a new or deeper religious experience involves cultivating a new spiritual discipline or doing a traditional discipline like prayer, meditation, reading a sacred text, or attending a liturgy in a new way or with a new attitude. We also talked about research findings into the positive mental and physical benefits of authentic spiritual practice. We also pointed out that spiritual practices directly question two of our culture's most cherished convictions: that natural science is the one and only way to the truth, and that acquiring more material possessions inevitably leads to happiness. And they challenge the basic security system of modern society with its thirst for total control and lust for possessions.

In the preceding chapter we spoke about two models for approaching life: hiking a trail and white-water canoeing. Hiking involves following a well-worn path, having a guidebook to guide your steps and a clear destination. White-water canoeing involves unexpected obstacles, unforeseen problems, and little control over the forces pushing you along. Life in the modern world is more like white-water canoeing: it is not realistic to expect a triptych or guidebook to guide us through life, or trail markers to show us every twist and turn. Instead we need coping skills and trustworthy companions.

Part of the point of this distinction between hiking and canoeing is to distinguish approaches to life that stress mastery and those that stress coping. Enough experience with a familiar trail and you can gain some mastery of it. But you cannot master life: you cannot conquer it. You can, however, learn coping skills. That is one of the psychological results of spiritual practices: they strengthen our sense of spiritual selfhood, thereby giving us the skills that enable us to live creatively and spiritually in the midst of life's cross-currents.

As a psychologist, one of the things that seems to me to create problems in the spiritual life is unrealistic expectations: that spiritual discipline or a firm faith will protect us from the threat of unemployment, the catastrophe of terminal illness, the turmoil of family problems. But then we are handed an unexpected pink-slip at work, or the oncologist tells us to prepare for the worst, or it is our child who is at the police station or our spouse who is talking about divorce. Then we feel betrayed by our faith and angry at God. We may never stop to consider whether our expectations were realistic or not.

Therefore, I want to speak for a spirituality that is both realistic and transformative.

Stress and Coping

Thinking about spiritual practice and spiritual selfhood in terms of the psychology of coping can, I think, point the way to a spirituality that is both realistic and transformative. Research in psychology defines coping as the op-posite of stress. Stress is a word that many patients these days use to describe their situation: not depressed or anxious as much as stressed, stressed out, overwhelmed, out of control. Without going into the whole discussion of the physiology of stress, I can simply say that stressful situations reduce our im-mune system functioning, increase the burden on our cardiovascular system, and deplete the body of certain essential chemicals. Under stressful condi-tions we are more apt to catch colds and the flu and other more serious ill-nesses, to suffer cardiovascular problems, to be more susceptible to allergies.

For example, students while taking exams had a much lower than normal production of cells essential to the functioning of the immune system, and the cells they did produce were less vigorous in fighting infections. Likewise those continually caring for relatives with Alzheimer's disease suffered seri-ous reductions in the efficiency of their immune systems. Long-term stresses like divorce, bereavement, or unemployment compromised the immune sys-tem more than did short-term stresses. And stress resulting from interper-sonal problems had a more serious effect than stress caused by impersonal events, like natural disasters.

In the 1970s two researchers, Thomas Holmes and Richard Rahe, devel-oped a scale to measure stress. After three decades of research a clear corre-lation has been established and re-established between higher scores on this "Holmes-Rahe Stress Scale" (indicating more stress) and more susceptibility to virtually any type of physical illness. The more stressed you are, the more you are apt to get sick. Period.

But once this pattern was established, then, of course, exceptions were found. Not every stressed-out person got sick. I can remember how this re-search was reported in the media. It followed a cycle that the media always follows in reporting medical information—a cycle that does so much dam-age to our understanding of issues of health and sickness. At first every new finding is touted as a breakthrough (perhaps THE breakthrough)—be it a new drug or surgical procedure, a new nutritional finding, or a new epi-demiological study on the connection between behavior or stress and dis-ease. The public is encouraged to think of every new discovery as a kind of magic bullet. But then more extensive and detailed studies find a more com-plex picture—the miracle drug has unhappy side-effects (all drugs do, after all), some patients of the new surgical procedure develop complications (of course, even the most "routine" surgery is a complicated affair), or (in this case) not everyone who is under stress comes down with some illness. And the implication is then that the original discovery was seriously flawed because it fell short of our wish for a magic bullet that was reinforced by all the media hype. And so the real truth and benefit of a new medical discovery can easily get lost in the public's wave of disillusionment.

Later research has certainly found that not every stressed person gets sick. Why not, if there is such a tight connection between stress and illness? Because later research also found that there are significant buffers against the harmful effects of stress. These do not reduce the stress itself but rather they reduce the deleterious effects of stress on the body. Following are some of these buffers.

First, social support. The isolated lives that many in modern society lead is a major epidemiological factor. Those who live alone or have few friends or little intimate contact with others have a higher incidence of almost every physical and mental disorder. Studies comparing two groups that are equal on levels of stress, diet, smoking, and personality find that the group whose members have close friends, frequent contacts with family, and other people whom they can call on are much less apt to get sick despite their stresses or unhealthy lifestyles. Those with social support who are also involved in the long-term care of Alzheimer's patients or others with chronic conditions suffer a less severe decline in their immune system functioning than those caregivers without social support.

The second buffer is the possession of coping skills. Patients with stress-related disorders who undergo a program of stress management in which they are taught relaxation techniques, are encouraged to exercise regularly, and are given an opportunity to express pent-up emotions significantly improve their immune functioning even if the amount of stress in their life remains unchanged. Possessing these coping skills significantly reduces the effects of stress on the body.

A third buffer against the effects of stress involves the way in which we think about stressful situations. People who report feeling "overwhelmed" or "out to sea" in the face of life's stresses tend to have more serious health problems than those who feel that these same difficulties represent a challenge or an opportunity. Does giving a speech or taking an exam feel to you like a chance to demonstrate what you know or to get constructive feedback? Or do they feel like occasions to make a fool of yourself or be humiliated? It is not the event—the speech, or the exam, or the report due by a deadline—but rather how we think about them and what we tell ourselves about them that governs their impact on our physical and mental health. If we can see a stressful situation as a challenge or an opportunity, it will not affect our health as adversely as if we feel we are overwhelmed by it.

Another important factor regarding the way we may think about finding ourselves in the midst of a stressful situation concerns the amount of control we feel. Control does not mean omnipotence, an iron-fisted ability to impose our will on every event. The very search for that kind of invincibility itself adds to the stressful effects of a situation. Rather, control means that we feel we can have some impact on our circumstances or that we know we have the skills to handle them. Even animals being given a mild electric shock suffered a less significant decline in their immune system if they were given some control over the timing of the shocks but not their intensity or total number. If we can find ways to influence either the situations we are in or our reactions to them, we will be less affected by them. For example, changing the way we think about an unpleasant situation, from outrage to acceptance, or from being overwhelmed to being challenged, or knowing we have the resources to manage the situation, even if we cannot eliminate it, means we will be less "stressed" by it.

The fourth buffer against the ill effects of stress involves something discussed earlier—Antonovsky's research on coherence. Antonovsky showed that people who felt their lives had meaning and purpose and who had projects that they valued enough to commit themselves to were much less likely to suffer from virtually any physical or psychological disorder (except probably broken bones) than those who experienced their life as meaningless and without direction or purpose.

These four factors that reduce the effects of stress—social support, coping skills, thinking differently about the situation, and a sense of coherence—help us understand the crucial role that a spiritual practice can play in improving our health and well-being.

Spirituality and Coping

Clearly religious communities can serve as major sources of social support, and research has documented again and again the ways in which congregations support their members in times of personal and social disaster as well as providing the ongoing sense of belonging that has proven to be a major buffer against the deleterious health consequences of the stresses of modern life. On the other hand, research has also shown that religious communities that ostracize their members in times of crisis or teach the victims to blame themselves inevitably make bad situations worse. If someone is attempting to cope with a personal or family crisis or a medical difficulty and their local congregation shuns them, psychologically they would be better off alone than belonging to such a group. Or if their theology tells them that such times of difficulty are their own fault or the result of the wrath of God, their ability to handle the situation and even grow from it will be severely weakened. Such people come looking for bread and receive only a stone, the weight of which only adds to their burdens. So religious community can be a very positive (or very negative) factor in handling stress. But those who belong to benign and supportive congregations, regardless of religious ideology, possess a powerful resource for personal well-being.

In times of crisis we are better off if we feel we have the resources needed to manage the situation. A well-developed spiritual practice contains many elements that can serve as powerful managers of stress and agents of coping. Countless studies have shown how meditation produces the kind of deep relaxation that is one of life's most powerful antidotes to stress. Other studies have revealed the ways in which the practice of prayer enables people to cope with life's minor hassles and major catastrophes in creative and positive ways. Feeling you are working together with God to solve a problem or sensing a greater presence so that you are not alone, or being able to call upon a greater presence that can empower you in the face of life's challenges—research has shown that these common religious experiences, as well as many others, are consistently linked to resiliency in the face of crisis and psychologically beneficial responses to life's challenges.

In addition, throughout human history, religion is clearly the primary source for what Antonovsky calls coherence—the awareness that life makes sense, has meaning, and contains projects of value—that is a significant buffer against physical and psychological illness. Thus a meaningful spiritual practice, not just a mindless repetition of religious cliches or liturgical forms, can be a major source of resiliency and hardiness in the face of life's major and minor stresses.

In all of these ways—providing social support, teaching meditative techniques, giving people constructive ways to think about life, supplying a sense of meaning and coherence—research finds that spiritual commitments and practices are a major antidote to the stresses of modern life. Such conclusions should bolster the faith of those who already derive meaning and pleasure from their spiritual disciplines. Such findings might also encourage those who are skeptical but find themselves intrigued by the practice of spiritual disciplines to try with an open mind meditation, reading books about the spiritual journey, and participating in the liturgical life of a religious congregation.

Rather than promising to shield us from life's vicissitudes, a realistic understanding of the value of spiritual discipline will emphasize the many specific ways that consistent spiritual practice will provide us with the skills necessary to handle the cross-currents of life.

Beyond Coping

But this is as far as psychology can take us. It can demonstrate (in a culture that needs demonstrations) through elaborate studies what every committed spiritual person knows—that religious belief and practice have a supportive, enhancing, affirming impact on our lives. Psychology can also spell out some of the things that go into making religious practice either a positive force (providing coherence, meaning, values, social support, coping skills) or a negative one (deploying judgment, ostracism, or shame). All this is good as far as it goes.

But I suspect at this point many feel that something is missing. What is it?

One of the things missing is the transformative power of religion. Psychology speaks of religion as providing support, but many religions are not content with only support. Most traditions also seek transformation individually and socially.

Psychology and medicine tend to think of problems in terms of "homeostasis"—a balanced state, a steady state, or the normal state. Health represents the status quo, the absence of symptoms. Disease destroys this balanced, functional state. Treatment restores it.

But spiritual practice is not primarily about removing symptoms, either physical or psychological ones. Spiritual teachings are not content with only coping with life, with only a return to a homeostatic condition. These are important and necessary for human fulfillment, but they are not spiritually sufficient. Spirituality looks for transformation.

Psychology underscores the fact that transformation comes primarily from experience. A good theory is not sufficient. A good theory should lead to a good practice that leads to a new experience. In psychotherapy, just having a good theory is not enough. Psychotherapy is not about teaching the patient a new theory of human nature. It is about giving the patient a new experience of herself in the context of a new and different kind of relationship with the therapist. The theory is only helpful if it leads to new practices—new ways of relating to one's self, new ways of acting at home and on the job; new ways of relating that bring forth new experiences of one's self and one's relation to others. That is to say, it is putting new insight and understanding into practice that brings forth change and transformation.

Likewise, having a good theory about God will not lead to further spiritual development unless that theory is also a guide to practice, to doing something new or doing something familiar in a new way. So again, in the spiritual journey, theory should give rise to practice—in this case, perhaps, meditation, prayer, liturgical participation, feeding the hungry, visiting the sick, reaching out to the distraught. And practice should generate new experiences—a deeper realization of the presence of God, a new awareness of places of alienation and falling short and their cure, new vistas of peace and tranquility, a greater appreciation of religious community. These new experiences, and others like them, are the heart of transformation.

So at the end we come again to the question of how spiritual practices are transformative. To that we now turn.

Opening Pandora's Box

The ancient Greeks told a story about a girl named Pandora who was given a beautiful box to look at and play with, but she was told never to open it. Of course curiosity got the best of her. She opened it, and a swarm of demons flew out. That, the story concludes, is how evil was released into the world.

Something like that happens when we begin meditating. As the earliest spiritual masters of Christianity knew, as soon as we begin to quiet our mind, it seems like all the demons of our life are set free. We immediately recall that word said in anger to a friend that we still regret. Next comes the favor we agreed to do and then neglected. Then there's the time we manipulated someone else to get something for ourselves. And we saw someone falsely accused and unfairly treated and we didn't speak up for them. Half-forgotten lies and disagreement flood our minds like newly liberated evil spirits.

As soon as I begin to concentrate on my breathing, in and out, a space is opened up into which fears and anxieties rush. The phone bill; did I forget to pay it? I am flying across the country to a meeting next week; will the plane be safe? The car; is it time for its servicing? My sweetheart; is she going to leave me? My younger colleague died suddenly last month; when will my time come?

Meditation inevitably raises the question: How much anxiety, how much honesty, can I tolerate?

Learning meditation is not only learning about posture and breathing and the use of mantras. Learning meditation also means learning how to work with the anxieties, dreads, and memories arising in the course of meditation. Pure mindfulness meditation counsels simply observing and so gradually detaching from them. The psychologist in me feels that method alone may keep me from learning some things about myself that attending to and exploring these eruptions from my unconscious might teach me.

These eruptions of thought and feeling are precious messengers from within me, telling me about my motivations, desires, wishes, fears, and dreads. What I am not aware of cannot be faced, and so cannot be changed. Now, in meditation, I become aware of these disowned thoughts and feelings and experiences. Now they are present in a way that I might wonder about them. When have I felt such things before? Some feelings may go back to what the psychologist Erik Erikson called "the darkness of the first days of existence." How have I handled such feelings in the past? Have I suppressed them? Blamed myself for having them? How have they interfered with my life so far? Have they poisoned my relationships? Have they led me into jobs and relationships and other decisions that I have later regretted?

This is one of the ways a meditative practice can be transformative: forcing us to face previously disowned and hidden aspects of ourselves. But not only face them. By itself such a process might easily lead to more confusion and self-blame. In meditation we face these lost parts of ourselves in a reflective and detached mood. We confront them in the context of an awareness of a greater, spiritual presence. Can we meet them with the love and forgiveness of Jesus? Can we meet them with the compassion of the Buddhas and Bodhisattvas? Can we hold together these swirling inner demons with our meditative awareness of our unity with the center of the cosmos? If so, we are in a better position to learn from them, to gain perspective on them, and so gradually they may relinquish their power in our lives.

Early Christian spiritual masters and many Buddhists teach that it is precisely these fears and anxieties that keep us from encountering the Logos or Buddha nature within. Coming to terms with the interior forces that propel our actions and deflect our best intentions is not only a matter of psychological healing, but also a matter of spiritual growth and transformation; coming back again and again to our breath and our breathing and our meditative routine; returning time and time again to face ourselves. This is part of the courage and discipline of the spiritual life. At these times I am reminded of a Japanese saying that guides me in my martial arts training: "He who conquers others is strong; he who conquers himself is truly mighty."

A New Way of Knowing

But what exactly is transformed through spiritual practices? Psychotherapy usually seeks to transform an individual's ways of thinking, feeling, and behaving. After a successful treatment, the former patient can now freely socialize instead of being paralyzed with anxiety; can now clearly and directly communicate with friends and family instead of approaching them in an angry and defensive way; can now realistically assess his own strengths and weaknesses instead of continually thinking of himself as the lowest of the low or as the center of the universe. Through therapy, the *content* of a person's thinking and acting has changed: new behaviors have been added to her repertoire, new ways of thinking and feeling toward herself and others have replaced outmoded ones.

Spiritual practices may also add new thoughts, feelings, and actions to our lives: meditation may supply new moments of calm and tranquility; devotional reading may bring new insights into the nature of God; a compelling experience of worship may motivate our reaching out to the sick and suffering. But I want to suggest that the real transformation brought about by spiritual discipline is less in the content of *what* we know and more in *how* we know.

In this culture most, if not all, of our knowledge comes through abstraction. I stand back and look at a tree or a rock or a cell (or maybe another person) and study them from a distance. I abstract myself out of the situation as much as possible in order to be objective. As much as possible I focus all my attention on the external characteristics of the object: the kind of material that the tree or the rock consists of, the structures of the cell and how they function, the condition of the person's skin or the functioning of their organs (if I am doing a medical diagnosis). We call this the scientific method. It has been extremely fruitful in the twentieth century. So fruitful that many of our contemporaries think it is the only path to knowledge.

For some people religious knowing is like this, too. The creeds and teachings of the Christian tradition, the texts of the Bible, the ideas of inspired teachers and thinkers give us abstract or objective knowledge about God and His (in such contexts God is usually a "He") nature and will or the ultimate nature and destiny of the human spirit. I can study them much as I would a textbook in physics. If I agree with what these religious sources say, then I am said to "have faith." If I don't accept them, then I call myself a "nonbeliever." For those who take this approach, being a Christian means knowing new things (the existence of God, the destiny of the soul, the meaning of a text) in the same old way.

From a psychological standpoint, the problem with this approach to religious knowing is that it rarely produces transformation. People can accept certain ideas about the truth of a sacred text or the existence of an ultimate reality or a personal God and remain basically the same. This is because such notions are held in an abstract way, like the propositions of physics. They are held in a way that is impersonal and keeps them at a distance.

Earlier, when I was discussing the Christian doctrine of the Trinity and the Buddhist idea of emptiness, I suggested that these were not concepts to be debated. Rather I called them contemplative strategies. By this I mean we are to approach them by meditating on them (or some other spiritual text or image), reflecting on them within a relaxed and tranquil mind-set, and paying attention to what happens to us when we do that: What sensations are evoked in our bodies as we say to ourselves, "Lord Jesus have mercy upon me" in time to our breathing? What emotions are stirred within us as we focus our attention on the crucifix (or a picture of the Bodhisattva of compassion)? What memories come forth as we reflect on the miracles of Jesus (or the enlightenment of Siddhartha)? What images streak through our minds, what insights come to us unbidden as we envision the Lotus flower opening or the three intersecting circles of the Holy Trinity? Can we sense the power of the universal Logos, the Tao of Christ, rise within us?

Such contemplative knowing is the opposite of abstract knowing. Contemplative knowing is knowing by personal participation. Bodies, feelings, fleeting images, unformed ideas—all the things left out in abstract ways of knowing—all play a part in contemplative knowing. And since contemplative knowing reawakens dimensions of ourselves and facets of our experience formerly ignored or suppressed, it is genuinely transformative.

Such a way of knowing often seems unfamiliar, even suspicious, to us because we have been brought up to champion abstraction as the only sure way to knowledge. To undertake such a process requires discipline. Not just strolling through the woods or along the beach, but rather walking in a tranquil but mindful way—paying attention to the smells and sounds, the brush of wind against your face and arms, the arising mental pictures—and allowing one's self to be engulfed by the experience of being there. Not just sitting passively in the pew but participating in the liturgical activity of a community at worship: paying attention to the bodily sensations and mental pictures evoked by the reading of a sacred text; to the physical and emotional responses to music; to which words strike you today; to the milieu created by flickering candles, pictures and statures, the smell of incense. Again, it involves allowing oneself to be engulfed by the experience of being there; or sitting comfortably and focusing on the cycle of your breathing, watching your thoughts as they pass from one side of your mind to the other; or repeating "Jesus Christ, have mercy upon me" in tune with your heart. When you stop and stand up, how are you different? How do you experience your mind now? What is going on in your body? Such contemplative knowing requires discipline.

That is why contemplative knowing is not a flight of fancy like a daydream or a short-cut around rigorous thought for the mentally lazy. It is not simply the cultivation of interesting experiences for their own sake. It requires as much discipline as learning experimental design or statistical analysis or improving your tennis game. It demands learning to pay attention, especially to fragments of experience that we might have been conditioned to ignore. It requires training to quiet the mind and relax the body (even if one is out walking or practicing a martial art) so that new physical and mental sensations can make themselves felt. It involves being able to reflect back on the insights gained and experiences evoked in order to integrate them into your life and your ongoing practice. Thus contemplative knowing utilizes critical reasoning, but as a servant of transformation and deeper knowing, not as a master to which all of life must simply submit.

Deeper contemplative knowing is not a momentary "peak experience." It is a source of ongoing insight into the ultimate nature of reality. Insight means to "see into," and through the practices of contemplative knowing we come to "see into" the depths of the cosmos. There we find the Tao of Christ "in whom all things were created . . . in whom all things are held together" (Colossians). We see that the universe has the form it does because of the Logos (or the dharmakaya) within it—the primal and immaterial spring from which matter arises. The material cosmos is constantly pulsating with vitality and continually undergoing transformations. The presence of the Logos animates the physical world, for the Logos is the spiritual source from which the material world erupts. Contemplative knowing enables us to see both the continual changes and fluctuations that make transitory and fragile everything to which we try to cling, and also the ultimate spiritual ground from which everything emerges and to which it returns.

Earlier we discussed the existence of a God beyond negation and affirmation, beyond existence and non-existence. How could such a God be known, since, we are inclined to think, knowing involves precisely the process of affirming some things as true ("This is an oak tree outside my window") and negating others as false ("No, there are no such animals as unicorns")? Obviously such a God cannot be known by the same process by which we affirm or deny the existence of physical objects like trees and unicorns, since such a God is precisely not one physical object among others. And if one's faith (and that is what it is) is that this abstract way of knowing is the only way of knowing, then obviously such a God cannot be known at all.

Contemplative disciplines, however, open us up to other sources of information and other ways of knowing. Contemplative disciplines nurture our dormant intuitive facility. They create in us the possibility of a way of knowing in which paradoxes (like the divine reality being beyond affirmation and negation, or One God as a Trinity, or emptiness as form and form as emptiness) can be the source of genuine insight and knowledge. They loosen our attachments to traditional forms and concepts (including religious ones), enabling us to let go of them and pass beyond them (as described in *The Cloud of Unknowing*). Thus these disciplines facilitate our entrance into that cloud of unknowing in which such a divine reality can be known. Contemplative disciplines are transformative because they go beyond simply knowing new things in the same old way, to opening up new ways of knowing and lost dimensions of our experience. Contemplative knowing is not a substitute or replacement for abstract knowing. Rather it is a supplement and complement to it. Both are necessary for the fully human life.

The irony here is that the only way you can know that this is true is by committing yourself to the practices of contemplative knowing and trying them out. Basic truths about life are like that. I cannot prove to you in some abstract way that running or mountain climbing can be exhilarating, that scientific investigation can be productive, that it is better to live with intimate relationships in your life than to live an isolated life, that spiritual practice can lead to new truths. You can take my word for it or observe the results in someone else's life and so have the kind of secondhand knowledge discussed earlier. But to know such things for yourself you have to commit yourself to them and live them out. They are only known to be true by practicing them. Those who will not or cannot undertake a spiritual practice should not wonder that spiritual experiences pass them by and that religious talk makes no sense to them.

The Mirror of God

In his second letter to the Corinthians, the apostle Paul refers to an account in the Hebrew scriptures about how, when Moses came down from Mt. Sinai and from seeing God, his face was so bright that he had to put a veil over it. Then Paul comments on this story by saying,

> Indeed every time the Law of Moses is read, a veil lies over the mind of the hearer. But the scripture says, whenever one turns to the Lord, the veil is removed. Now when speaking of the Lord, this passage is referring to the Spirit and where the Spirit is, there is freedom. And we, with unveiled face, beholding and reflecting the glory of the Lord, are being transformed into his image, going from glory to glory in the power of the Spirit.

The Greek word at the center of Paul's commentary means both to behold and to reflect, like looking into a mirror, and I have put both meanings into my translation here. We are back at the end to where we began—with the importance of presence. Beholding and reflecting the divine presence, we are gradually being changed. A spiritual practice—whether meditation, centering prayer, *Lectio Divina,* active imagination, liturgical worship, or something else done in a disciplined way—is one that enables us to behold the divine presence and to reflect it in our lives.

When we face these spiritual experiences, according to Paul's discussion, we experience a "mirroring"—a beholding and reflecting of our image in the light of the divine presence. To a psychologist, the experience of mirroring is one of the most basic human experiences. We are not born with a sense of who we are. Rather as infants we develop a sense of ourselves by seeing ourselves reflected back, mirrored back to us in the responses of those around us. If the mirror is cracked, if parents or other caretakers reflect back a harsh, critical, distorted image, the child will grow up thinking of herself as living under some condemnation, as a failure, as grotesque in some way. Our self-image is really a reflected image. Mirroring and being mirrored is one of the most formative experiences in human development.

And later in life mirroring can be one of the most transformative experiences in our ongoing development. The child diminished after years of failure is suddenly turned around when a new teacher mirrors back to her talents and abilities she had never before seen in herself. Research on kids who "beat the odds" (that is, kids who everyone gave up on in school and later became productive persons) almost always finds that some adult—teacher, coach, grandparent, clergyperson—took an interest in them and reflected back to them a new image of who they are.

Paul is suggesting here that when we encounter the presence of God, a further mirroring is taking place: we behold and reflect the divine presence and we see the image of God within us reflected back in the divine image. In the communion liturgy, Christians take up a body that was broken and see their brokenness and that of their world reflected back. When they stare into the depths of the blood-red chalice they see their wounds mingled with Jesus'. Wounds must be healed by wounds. That was the wisdom of God in the Incarnation of Jesus. Patients seek until they find a therapist who they think will understand, whose experience is similar enough to their own (it does not have to be exactly the same), for a mirroring to take place in which the patient experiences their life story reflected back to them with new empathy and understanding.

As we read the scriptures and put ourselves in the place of King David, who flagrantly disobeyed and remained accepted; of Peter, who betrayed and was forgiven; of the disciples who feared the storm and found in it a place of peace and calm; of the prostitute who received a blessing; of doubting Thomas, who saw something unforeseen and unexpected; as we walk along the beach or through the woods and sense the One who is present in and through the world; as we touch a friend and let ourselves be touched by their friendship; as we bring our joys and sorrows, insights and questions, celebrations and losses to be joined with the body that was broken and the blood that was spilled, through such ongoing practices the veil is lifted and, beholding and reflecting, mirroring and being mirrored, we are gradually transformed into the divine image from glory to glory.

Epilogue

This is a book about how lives are changed. But reading this book will not change your life. The only thing that will do that is committing or recommitting yourself to a spiritual practice or practices. This book can provide plenty of reasons for doing that. It can give you an understanding of what spiritual practice is. But it cannot do the work you must do yourself. I sometimes say to patients that I can write the prescription but I can't take it for them. This is another instance in which spiritual practice is like psychotherapy.

So we have now come to the end of all the studies of the beneficial mental and physical effects of spiritual practice. We have now finished all the accounts of other people's (including my own) religious experiences. We have now completed our analysis of modern culture and its impact on our spiritual search. We now leave behind all the speculations about the nature of the Divine Abyss and the presence and absence of the One beyond affirmation and negation.

All that is left now is the meditation seat. Waiting for us to sit. To attend to our breathing. To softly repeat words of meaning as we breathe in and breathe out.

All that is left now is the woods, the seaside, the park. Waiting for us to walk there. To absorb the smells and sounds, to feel our body move, to gradually sense the presence that dwells there.

All that is left now is the congregation. Waiting for us to come. To take our place. To listen to the words. To sing or chant or bow or dance. To move, to see, to hear.

All that is left now is the neighbor. In the next cubicle. On the next street. Across the world. Suffering. Waiting for us to give them a hand. To give them a voice.

All that is left now is to begin. And begin again.

Bibliographical Essay

Given my desire to reach a wide audience, I did not want to cover the text with footnotes, although there is a lot of research and source material standing behind what I write here. Instead I have included this bibliographical section, which contains the sources I have used and some suggestions for further reading.

Chapter One: Faith as Practice

Further elaboration of the pragmatically based epistemology described in this chapter and in chapter four as it applies both to science and religion and the arguments supporting it can be found in J. Jones, 1981, *The Texture of Knowledge* (Lanham, MD: University Press of America). The ideas of Michael Polanyi are discussed there and found in his 1974 book *Personal Knowledge* (New York: Harper & Row).

The sources for this discussion of early Christian spirituality are: M. M. Funk, 1998, *A Mind at Peace* (Oxford: Lion Publishing); T. Merton, 1960, *The Wisdom of the Desert* (New York: New Directions); *The Philokalia*, 1995, Volumes 1–4 (London: Faber & Faber). Material on the "Jesus Prayer" can be found in the *Philokalia*. Quotations about the prayer of the heart are from St. Hesychios, "On watchfulness and holiness," *The Philokalia*, Vol. I, pp.162–163.

More information on Herbert Benson's research and the relaxation response can be found in H. Benson, 1975, *The Relaxation Response* (New York: William Morrow), and 1996, *Timeless Healing* (New York: Scribner).

A more extensive discussion of mindfulness meditation can be found in D. Goleman, 1977, *The Varieties of Meditative Experience* (New York: E. P. Dutton); A Deikman, 1982, *The Observing Self* (Boston: Beacon); Lama Govinda, 1974, *The Foundations of Tibetan Buddhism* (New York: Samuel Weiser); M. Epstein, 1995, *Thoughts Without a Thinker* (New York: Basic Books).

A good introduction to Thomas Keating's method of "centering prayer" can be found in his series of lectures "Contemplative Prayer," on tape from Sounds True Audio in Boulder, CO. A description of the monastic practice of *lectio divina* can be found in *In the Spirit of Happiness* by the monks of New Skete, 1999 (Boston: Little, Brown and Company).

A good introduction to Tibetan Buddhist meditation practices and views of the body can be found in J. Powers, 1995, *Introduction to Tibetan Buddhism* (Ithaca, NY: Snow Lion Press). A fine discussion of "ki" or "chi" in relation to both traditional Japanese practices and current views of the body can be found in Y. Yuaso, 1993, *The Body, Self-Cultivation, and Ki-Energy,* trans. S. Nagatomo and M. Hull (Albany, NY: SUNY Press). A description of some of the meditation practices associated with the "ki" or "chi" can be heard on K. Cohen, "The Power of Qi," on tape from Sounds True Audio, Boulder, CO. The quote about the Tao is from Lao Tzu, *The Way of Life,* trans. R. Blakney, 1955 (NY: Mentor Books).

A fuller discussion of the Logos theology in early Christianity can be found in J. Jones, 1984, *The Redemption of Matter* (Lanham, MD: University Press of America) and R. A. Norris, 1965, *God and World in Early Christianity* (New York: Seabury Press).

Chapter Two: The Paradoxical Presence

The quotation is from Martin Buber, 1970, *I and Thou,* trans. W. Kaufman (New York: Scribner, pp. 158–159) and is slightly altered. The account of a contemporary religious experience is from J. W. Jones, 1995, *In The Middle of This Road We Call Our Life* (San Francisco: Harper San Francisco) and originally is from F. C. Happold, 1963, *Mysticism* (New York: Penguin Books).

For more on the task of psychoanalysis in relation to religion, see J. Jones, 1991, *Contemporary Psychoanalysis and Religion* (New Haven: Yale University Press). Excellent analyses of the psychology behind Freud's atheism can be found in W. W. Meissner, 1984, *Psychoanalysis and Religious Experience* (New Haven: Yale University Press) and A. M. Rizzuto, 1998, *Why Did Freud Reject God?* (New Haven: Yale University Press).

In the quotations from *The Cloud of Unknowing* in this chapter I have worked with two translations, *(The) Cloud of Unknowing*, 1981, ed. J. Walsh (New York: Paulist Press); and *(The)Cloud of Unknowing*, 1973, ed. W. Johnston (New York: Doubleday).

The reference to Karl Barth is to K. Barth, *Letter to the Romans.* Quotes from Thomas Merton are from T. Merton, 1973, *Contemplative Prayer* (London: Darton, Longman, Todd); T. Merton, 1966, *Conjectures of a Guilty Bystander* (Garden City, NY: Doubleday Publisher); T. Merton, 1961, *New Seeds of Contemplation* (New York: New Directions).

After having written this chapter, I was introduced to a book that covers much the same ground and provides another perspective on these topics, especially the desert spirituality and psychoanalysis: A. Jones (no relation), 1985, *Soul Making* (San Francisco: Harper & Row).

Chapter Three:
The Cross-Legged Buddha
and the Cross-Stricken Christ

This section on the early history of Buddhism and the development of the "Three Bodies" doctrine and the "Mind-only school" and the doctrine of the "tathagatagarbha" are drawn from the "Introduction" to *Buddhism in Practice,* 1995, edited by D. S. Lopez (Princeton, NJ: Princeton University Press); and P. Harvey, 1990, *An Introduction to Buddhism* (Cambridge: Cambridge University Press) and P. Williams, 1989, *Mahayana Buddhism* (London and New York: Routledge Press). A further discussion of the Bodhisattva tradition can be found in Chun-fang Yu, 2001, *Kuan-yin: The Chinese transformation of Avalokitesvara* (New York: Columbia University Press). I want to thank Professor Yu for calling my attention to the story of the Bodhisattva "Non-disparaging" in the Lotus Sutra and for her careful reading and helpful commentary on this chapter.

Much of the material on the "Middle Way" and especially the tradition of Nagarjuna is taken from R. Thurman, 1984, *The Central Philosophy of Tibet: A Study and Translation of Jey Tsong Khapa's Essence of True Eloquence* (Princeton, NJ: Princeton University Press), especially Thurman's "Introduction." An excellent overview of the Tibetan tradition can be found in J. Powers, 1995, *Introduction to Tibetan Buddhism* (Ithica, NY: Snow Lion Publications).

In the discussion of the development of early Christianity, I do not intend to enter into the currently hot controversy about the historical Jesus. For those who want to go there, a good, accessible introduction to the scholarly debate can be found in M. Borg and N. T. Wright, 1999, *The Meaning of Jesus: Two Visions* (San Francisco: Harper San Francisco). An excellent, easily understandable account of Jesus and early Christianity can be found in T. Cahill, 1999, *Desire of the Everlasting Hills* (New York: Doubleday). A good introduction to the development of the early church's thinking about Jesus can be found in R. A. Norris, 1965, *God and World in Early Christianity* (New York: Seabury Press). I have covered some of this material earlier in another context, in J. W. Jones, 1984, *The Redemption of Matter* (Lanham, MD: University Press of America).

The Buddhist-Christian discussion that forms the larger context for this chapter has been going on a long time. A good historical overview can be found in W. Lai and M. von Bruck, 2001, *Christianity and Buddhism: A Multi-cultural History of Their Dialogue* (New York: Orbis), although its very academic style does not spare the reader. Clear and provocative examples of the philosophical-theological discussion between the traditions can be found in J. Cobb, 1982, *Beyond Dialogue: Toward a Mutual Transformation of Christianity and Buddhism* (Philadelphia: Fortress Press) and J. Cobb and C. Ives (eds.), 1990, *The Emptying God* (New York: Orbis Books). Books from the Buddhist side include, T. N. Hanh, 1995, *Living Buddha, Living Christ* (New York: Riverhead Books) and the Dali Lama, 1996, *The Good Heart: A Buddhist Perspective on the Teachings of Jesus* (Boston: Wisdom Publishing). Books from the Christian side include two by William Johnston, 1981, *The Mirror Mind* (San Francisco: Harper & Row) and 1971, *Christian Zen* (New York: Harper & Row); and, on a more theological level, J. Cobb, 1975, *Christ in a Pluralistic Age* (Philadelphia: Westminster Press). Examples of the kind of fruitful discussion that can occur between practitioners of Christian and Buddhist spiritual disciplines can be found in W. Mitchell and J. Wiseman, 1999, *The Gethsemane Encounter* (New York: Continuum) and S. Walker, 1987, *Speaking of Silence: Christians and Buddhists on the Contemplative Way* (New York: Paulist Press).

The comparison of Buddhist and Christian iconography—Buddha in nirvana and Jesus in agony—was suggested by a passage in N. Smart, 1981, *Beyond Ideology* (New York: Harper & Row). The model of early development as a process of "separation-individuation" is based on the work of Margaret Mahler and is described in S. Blank and R. Blank, 1979, *Ego Psychology, Vol. II* (New York: Columbia University Press). This discussion of the use of mindfulness meditation and gestalt techniques in therapy is drawn from: S. Boorstein, 1983, "The use of bibliotherapy and mindfulness meditation in a psychiatric setting," *Journal of Transpersonal Psychology,* 15:173–179; S. Boorstein, 1981, *Transpersonal Psychotherapy* (Palo Alto, CA: Science and Behavior Books); A. Deikman, 1982, *The Observing Self* (Boston: Beacon); J. Fagen and I. Shepherd, 1970, *Gestalt Therapy* (New York: Harper & Row); F. Perls, 1971, *Gestalt Therapy Verbatim* (New York: Bantam Books); E. Polster and M. Polster, 1974, *Gestalt Therapy Integrated* (New York: Vintage Books); N. Thera, 1969, *The Heart of Buddhist Meditation.* (London: Rider & Co.).

Chapter Four:
Christian Spirituality and Modern Society

Research on religion and well being can be found in D. G. Meyers, 1993, *The Pursuit of Happiness* (New York: Avon). K. Chamberlain and S. Zika, 1988, "Religiosity, Life Meaning and Well Being," *Journal for the Scientific Study of Religion* 27:411–42. R. A. Witter, W. A. Stock, M. A. Okum, M. J. Haring, 1985, "Religion and Subjective Well Being in Adulthood: a Quantitative Synthesis," *Review of Religious Research* 26:332–42. St. George and McNamara, 1984, "Religion, Race, and Psychological Well-Being," *Journal for the Scientific Study of Religion.* 22(3):239–252. Willits and Crider, 1988, "Religion and Well-Being," *Review of Religious Research* 29(3): 281–294. Koenig, et al., 1988, "Religion and Well-Being in Later Life," *The Gerontologist* 28(1): 18–29. Peterson and Roy, 1985, "Religiosity, Anxiety, and

Meaning and Purpose: Religion's Consequences for Psychological Well-Being," *Review of Religious Research* 27(1): 49–62; Carson, et al., 1988, "Hope and its Relationship to Spiritual Well-Being," *Journal of Psychology and Theology* 16(2): 159–167.

Quotation about "faith in a supernatural order" is from M. Csikszentmihalyi, 1999, "If We Are So Rich, Why Aren't We Happy?" *American Psychologist* 54: 824.

Research on the importance of meaning for human happiness is from A. Antonovsky, 1987, *Unraveling the Mystery of Health* (San Francisco: Jossey-Bass); P. Wong and P Frey, 1998, *The Human Quest for Meaning* (Mahwah, NJ: Lawrence Erlbaum); C. Park and S. Folkman, 1997, "The Role of Meaning in the Context of Stress and Coping," *General Review of Psychology* 2: 115–144.

For research on the failure of materialistic pursuits alone to provide lasting happiness, see M. Csikszentmihalyi, 1999, "If We Are So Rich, Why Aren't We Happy?" *American Psychologist*, 54/10:823, and D. Myers, 2000, "The Funds, Friends, and Faith of Happy People," *American Psychologist* 55/1: 34–43.

For research on religion and health, see: C. D. Batson and W. L. Ventis, 1982, *The Religious Experience* (New York: Oxford) (chapter 7, review of research on religion and mental health); T. Chamberlain and C. Hall, 2000, *Realized Religion* (Philadelphia: Templeton Press); H. Koenig, 1997, *Is Religion Good for Your Health?* (New York: Haworth Press); H. Koenig, M. McCullough, and D. Larson, 2001, *Handbook of Religion and Health* (New York: Oxford University Press); D. Larson, et. al, 1997, *Scientific Research on Spirituality and Health*, available from the National Institute for Healthcare Research, Rockville, MD; D. Mathews, D. Larson, et al., 1993–1997, *The Faith Factor,* Volumes I, II, III, IV, available from the National Institute for Healthcare Research, Rockville, MD. Critical evaluations of this research that still generally support the findings discussed here can be found in T. Plante and A. Sherman, 2001, *Faith and Health* (New York: Guilford). Of course there is a little-noticed irony in this research: it seems that the benefits of a spiritual practice primarily accrue to those who practice their spirituality for its own sake and not for the sake of some benefit beyond just the practice itself (the so-called intrinsic religious practitioners as opposed to the "extrinsic practitioner" who looks to some material or social benefit from their religion). That is why I never prescribe a religious practice to a patient. One cannot prescribe a spiritual practice to a patient for the sake of its health benefits, for then the practice would seem to be "extrinsic" and therefore less efficacious.

Additional discussion of the question of a unique role for religion in human health can be found, in addition to the above references, in J. Levin, 1996, "How Prayer Heals: A Theoretical Model," *Alternative Therapies* 2(1):66–73, and H. Benson, 1996, *Timeless Healing* (New York: Scribner).

On the scientific view of the world as meaningless, see for example, S. Weinberg, 1993, *The First Three Minutes* (New York: Basic Books); J. Monod, 1971, *Chance and Necessity* (New York: Random House). My own approach to the relationship between science and religion is spelled out further in two books: J. Jones, 1981, *The Texture of Knowledge* (Lanham, MD: University Press of America), J. Jones, 1984, *The Redemption of Matter* (Lanham: University Press of America).

The idea that modern culture creates a "cocoon of security" by repressing certain "existential" concerns is taken from A. Giddens, 1991, *Modernity and Self-Identity* (Cambridge: Polity Press); a book that was very influential on my thinking. Before that a similar argument was made by P. Berger, 1967, *The Sacred Canopy* (New York: Doubleday-Anchor).

Sigmund Freud's attack on religion can be found in 1961, *The Future of an Illusion* (New York: Norton); Albert Ellis's, in 1971, *The Case Against Religion: A Psychotherapist's View* (New York: Institute for Rational Living) and "Psychotherapy and Astheistic Values," *Journal of Consulting and Clinical Psychology* 48: 635–639.

The claim that religious believers survived better under the harsh circumstances of the Nazi death camps is based on the research of Paul Marcus. See, for example, P. Marcus, 1998, "The Religious Believer, the Psychoanalytic Intellectual and the Challenge of Sustaining the Self in the Concentration Camps," *Journal for the Psychoanalysis of Culture & Society* 3/1, 61–75. A similar claim underlies the work of Victor Frankl; see for example, 1963, *Man's Search for Meaning* (New York: Washington Square Press).

Chapter Six: Spiritual Selfhood

The stories of patients referred to in this chapter are described in more detail in my book *In the Middle of This Road We Call Our Life.*

The quote from Robert Linder is from R. Linder, 1999, *The Fifty Minute Hour* (New York: Other Press).

Chapter Seven: The Mirror of God

Good basic reviews of the research on the physiology of stress can be found in S. Locke and D. Colligan, 1986, *The Healer Within* (New York: Dutton) and E. Sternberg, 2000, *The Balance Within* (New York: Freeman & Co.). The best discussion of religion's role in coping is K. Pargament, 1997, *The Psychology of Religion and Coping* (New York: Guilford).

For more on the transforming power of religious experience, see J. Jones, 2002, *Terror and Transformation: The Ambiguity of Religion in a Psychoanalytic Perspective* (London and New York: Routledge Press).

Index